Health *for* Life

Ages 4–7

Noreen Wetton
Trefor Williams

First published in 1989 by:
Thomas Nelson & Sons Ltd

Reprinted in 2000 by:
Nelson Thornes Ltd
Delta Place
27 Bath Road
CHELTENHAM
GL53 7TH
United Kingdom

05 / 10 9 8

A catalogue record of this book is available from the British Library

ISBN 0 17 423386 8

Printed in Croatia by Zrinski

Acknowledgments

The author and publishers wish to thank the following:

– Margaret Collins, former headteacher, Education Consultant, Visiting Fellow at
  Southampton University (Health Education Unit) and writer, for her considerable
  contribution to both the content and organisation of this book.

– the many UK primary schoolchildren and their teachers for taking part in research
  and for giving their valuable views on health, healthy lifestyles and healthy
  citizenship.

– the children of Larkrise School, Oxford, for participating in the photography in the
  book.

Contents

Introduction

Welcome to this new edition of *Health for Life*. There have been many changes in education, in the curriculum and in health education since the first edition was published. To reflect these changes, the whole of *Health for Life* has been rethought, reshaped, restructured and rewritten. The first edition of *Health for Life* was based on original child-centred research. We, the authors, have revisited this research for this new edition, and the results have had a considerable influence on the revised content and structure.

Health for Life enables you to develop and deliver a joint and spirally developed programme for Personal, Social and Health Education (PSHE) and Citizenship, Personal and Social Education (PSE) or Personal and Social Development (PSD) in your school. *Health for Life* responds to the challenge facing schools to '*give pupils the knowledge, skills and understanding they need to lead confident, healthy, independent lives and to become informed, active, responsible citizens*'. (National Curriculum, 2000)

The books provide a whole school, flexible response to the curriculum requirements and encourage involvement in the wider community. The books are closely linked to the non-statutory guidelines for Personal, Social and Health Education and Citizenship in England, the Personal and Social Education Framework in Wales (ACCAC, 2000) and the requirements of the Personal and Social Development 5–14 Guidelines in Scotland. These documents allow for a degree of flexibility in schools' responses, and this is reflected in the structure of *Health for Life* and the many ways in which it can be used effectively.

How *Health for Life* is organised

Health for Life is divided into two books, one for ages 4–7 and the other for ages 8–11, which correspond broadly to Key Stages 1 and 2 in the English and Welsh curriculum. In both books, material is presented to enable children to move through a broad-based healthy lifestyles programme and then to a consideration of three sensitive issues.

The structure diagram on page 6 shows how the elements of *Health for Life* work together.

Structure diagram for *Health for Life*

Two resource books
Health for Life Ages 4–7
Health for Life Ages 8–11

Each book contains two strands
Healthy Lifestyles
Sensitive Issues

Healthy Lifestyles
The key themes develop across the two books to encourage healthy lifestyle knowledge and skills

Sensitive Issues
Key themes:
• The world of drugs
• Keeping myself safe
• Me and my relationships

Action planners
These planners suggest a route through each of the Healthy Lifestyles and Sensitive Issues strands. They contain content boxes that form the starting points for the classroom activities

Classroom activities
A series of classroom activities based on the questions posed in the content boxes

Photocopiable activity sheets
These are linked to each of the three Sensitive Issues key themes

Classroom research strategy
The classroom research strategy underpins the philosophy and content of the material in these two books

How to use *Health for Life*

Health for Life is a flexible resource that can be used in many different ways. You may choose to:
- refer to the Classroom research strategy described in Appendix 1 and select the strategies and activities that are best matched to the children's needs
- bypass the research and go straight in through the Action planners
- match the Classroom activities to your school's pre-determined course structure.

The spiral curriculum model is at the heart of *Health for Life*, and it is, therefore, important to consider which topics have already been covered to ensure that knowledge is built on and skills developed.

Key themes

From our classroom research, drawing on a wide sample of children aged 4–7, we identified key themes for the two age ranges 4–5 and 6–7. These themes are:

Healthy Lifestyles

For ages 4–5 Growing and changing (pages 21–30)
      Keeping safe (pages 31–36)
      Medicines and drugs (pages 37–44)

For ages 6–7 Healthy lifestyles (pages 103–112)
      Healthy eating (pages 113–120)
      Feelings and relationships (pages 121–130)

Sensitive Issues

For ages 4–5 and 6–7
      The world of drugs (pages 46–59 and 132–147)
      Keeping myself safe (pages 60–79 and 148–171)
      Me and my relationships (pages 80–96 and 172–196)

Each key theme contains a planned route that enables teachers, and others involved, to see what the programme consists of and how they can work best with the school.

Each key theme begins with a clear summary outlining:
- the focus for teaching the theme
- key skills and competencies
- opportunities for Citizenship teaching
- links with children's literature.

Action planners

The Action planners, which occur throughout the Healthy Lifestyles and Sensitive Issues sections in the book, offer a reference framework that can be used by schools for planning. The Action planners consist of a series of structured questions in 'content boxes', which form a spiral curriculum of teaching and learning goals for ages 4–5 and then 6–7. These questions form the basis of the lesson plans.

There are two types of Action planners in the book:

Two, three-page Action planners for the Healthy Lifestyles section (see pages 18–20 for ages 4–5 and pages 100–102 for ages 6–7), each covering:

- Me and looking after myself
- Me, my family and my friends
- Me, my community and my environment.

Six, one-page Action planners for each of the Sensitive Issues sections (see pages 47, 61 and 81 for ages 4–5, and pages 133, 149 and 173 for ages 6–7). These cover three broad areas, and further develop the Healthy Lifestyles section of the book. These areas are:

- The world of drugs
- Keeping myself safe
- Me and my relationships.

Classroom activities

The structured questions in each content box are developed into a series of classroom activities that are easy to use and extend. Each activity can be developed into a lesson in itself. These activities have been trialled in classrooms and are illustrated with examples of how the children responded and contributed. Interactive methodologies and further Citizenship opportunities are also identified.

Reflection and action

Each key theme ends with a Reflection and action session, ideal for use as a class plenary session, reflecting on what has been learned in the course of the activities and what is necessary to put the learning into action in the children's everyday lives.

Photocopiable activity sheets

The 30 photocopiable activity sheets at the back of the book, linked to the three Sensitive Issues, support and extend the classroom activities, and can be used for differentiation.

Classroom research

Appendix 1 (pages 230–238) contains a series of open-ended research strategies. Teachers can take part in this research as a means of eliciting children's understanding of the health-related issues being explored in *Health for Life*. The first research strategy (see page 231) explores children's perceptions of what a healthy lifestyle is and provides starting points for the Healthy Lifestyles sections in this book. The other research strategies explore the issues of 'The World of Drugs', 'Keeping Myself Safe' and 'Me and My Relationships' from the Sensitive Issues section

The children's responses can then be used either as an assessment of needs or as a tool for evaluation. They should provide teachers with clearer insights into children's thinking about these particular issues. The results of the research could also be shared with parents, other teachers and community workers as an illustration of how children perceive PSHE and Citizenship, PSE or PSD issues.

Citizenship

The primary school Citizenship targets are tackled through the classroom activities within each theme (such as working in groups, coming to a consensus, respecting people's different views, decision-making, and problem-solving). The relevant Citizenship opportunities for each key theme are summarised in the Focus of teaching sections (at the beginning of each key theme).

Health for Life and the Primary School Curriculum

Throughout *Health for Life*, you will find opportunities to teach, extend and revise the skills, knowledge and understanding that children need in order to:

- *take and share responsibility*
- *feel positive about themselves*
- *take part in discussions*
- *make real choices*
- *meet and talk with people*
- *develop relationships through work and play*
- *consider social and moral dilemmas encountered in everyday life*
- *ask for help*
(National Curriculum, 2000)

- *have the appropriately positive regard for self and for others and their needs*
- *develop life skills to enable them to participate effectively and safely in society*
- *identify, review and evaluate the values that they and society hold, and recognise that these affect thoughts and actions*
- *take increasing responsibility for their own lives*
(Scottish Personal and Social Development 5–14 Guidelines, 1993)

- *equip pupils to be personally and socially effective*
- *develop pupils' self-esteem and personal responsibility*
- *prepare pupils for the challenges, choices and responsibilities of work and employment and lifelong learning*
- *empower pupils to participate in their communities as active citizens and to develop a global perspective*

- *assist pupils to live healthy and fulfilled lives*
- *foster and encourage positive attitudes and behaviour towards the environment and the principles of sustainable development locally, nationally and globally*

(Personal and Social Education Framework, ACCAC, 2000)

In both books, aspects of PSHE, Citizenship, PSE, PSD and emotional wellbeing are clearly identified. There are opportunities for extending work according to the school's individual programmes and policies – including those relating to drug education, relationships, sex education and personal safety.

England

The revised National Curriculum, published in September 1999, contained a new (non-statutory) Framework for Personal, Social and Health Education (PSHE) and Citizenship. This is a significant advance over the previous status of PSHE, when it was a cross-curricular theme as set out in Curriculum Guidance 5 (NCC, 1990). The report of the National Advisory Group on PSHE (DfEE, 1999) set out the ways in which PSHE makes a difference to pupils' learning and achievement:

- *motivation*
- *self-esteem*
- *responsibility*
- *key skills – such as communication, decision-making, managing change, working with others*
- *climate.*

Initial guidance issued by the QCA (April, 2000) on implementing the Framework for PSHE and Citizenship at Key Stages 1 and 2 advocated a whole school approach because *'pupil's personal and social development is influenced by many aspects of school life'*. It identifies three forms of curriculum provision:

- *discrete curriculum time*
- *teaching PSHE and citizenship through and in other subjects/curriculum areas*
- *through PSHE and citizenship activities and school events.*

The guidance suggests that a combination of these is needed in a whole school approach.

Wales

In January 2000 the Qualifications, Curriculum and Assessment Authority for Wales (ACCAC) published a Personal and Social Education Framework covering Key Stages 1 to 4. It states that *'in the school context, PSE comprises all that a school undertakes to promote the personal and social development of its pupils … not only in the classroom but also in other areas of school experience which are features of the ethos and community life of the school'.*

Scotland

The importance of Personal and Social Development (PSD) as a fundamental aspect of the education of the whole child is recognised in the Scottish Personal and Social Development 5–14 Guidelines. These state that pupils are required to *'increase their knowledge and understanding about themselves, others and their immediate environment and the world in which they live'.*

Personal development is seen as concerned with self-awareness and self-esteem, and social development is seen as concerned with interpersonal relationships, independence and interdependence. 'The Heart of the Matter' (SCCC, 1995) identifies five qualities as fundamental to PSD. They are:

- *respect and caring for self*
- *respect and caring for others*
- *a sense of social responsibility*
- *a commitment to learning*
- *a sense of belonging.*

Northern Ireland

The Educational (Cross Curricular) Themes state that pupils should:

- *learn to respect and value themselves and others*
- *appreciate the interdependence of people within society*
- *achieve their physical, psychological and social potential*
- *improve their self-knowledge and self-esteem*
- *develop knowledge and understanding of themselves and others as individuals.*

(DENI, 1992)

How *Health for Life* relates to the Health Promoting School and the National Healthy School Programme

The idea of the Health Promoting School, which first originated in 1984, is now an established concept in both the United Kingdom and Europe. The 'European Network of Health Promoting Schools' was launched in 1992, supported by the European Community, the World Health Organisation and the Council of Europe.

The National Healthy Schools Programme represents a partnership between Local Education and Health Authorities in England and is an integral part of the drive to improve health and education standards and to tackle health inequality. It is broadly based on a 'whole school, family and community' concept. It takes the view that, while much can be accomplished by schools themselves, this is greatly enhanced through working closely with children's families and the many organisations in their communities.

The National Healthy School Standard provides accreditation for these local partnership programmes. All schools have an opportunity to participate in such partnerships. The Standard will provide criteria by which the local Healthy Schools partnership can judge success in areas such as healthy eating and physical activity. Such partnerships must help schools meet legal demands, for example in sex and drug education, and follow the non-statutory guidelines.

Visitors from outside the school can also provide excellent support to PSHE and Citizenship programmes.

The basis of *Health for Life*

The key to solving any of our unhealthy lifestyle problems lies within each of us; it can be termed 'taking responsibility for our own behaviour'. It is, however, difficult for young children to take responsibility for their own health behaviour because they lack the necessary knowledge and skills, and are strongly influenced by their families. When developing healthy lifestyle messages for children, the support and active participation of parents and families are important. At the same time a growing sense of responsibility for their own behaviour should be instilled in young children themselves.

Healthy Lifestyles

Healthy lifestyle teaching for 4–7 year-olds includes topics such as making and keeping good relationships with others, eating a healthy diet, taking enough physical exercise, and keeping safe. Children begin to gain knowledge about these matters, for example about the dangers of smoking, but this needs to be matched by learning and practising skills that will later help them to make choices and decisions for themselves. The classroom activities provide plenty of opportunities for developing a programme to suit any class of young children.

Being in a class with children of the same age provides the children with exciting opportunities to discover their physical and emotional selves, how they look, how they know what goes on around them and how they feel about and react to others. This is also a critical period for their evolving self-image and a time to help them feel good about themselves. The ethos of *Health for Life* is one which develops in the child a sense of achievement through learning new skills and mastering new material. Many of the strategies in this book are ideal for introducing children to working in pairs and in small groups.

Sensitive Issues

This section tackles the range of issues that are sensitive to children, their families, the school, and the community. These issues have a strong influence on children's health, emotional wellbeing and behaviour as responsible young citizens.

Our research has shown that children think that sensitive topics include anything that makes them different, such as size, shape, family circumstances, lack of friends, family break-up, hurt feelings and being bullied. Parents, on the other hand, may think that sensitive issues are concerned with sex education, drug abuse, diseases, lack of motivation and child abuse. Most of these issues, together with their inter-related skills, are brought together and developed under three themes: 'The World of Drugs', 'Keeping Myself Safe' and 'Me and My Relationships'. These build on and extend the work of the Healthy Lifestyles section.

The World of Drugs

This section helps you to plan and implement a programme of drug education for your school. This section of the book helps young children to develop a balanced view of drugs, emphasising that drugs as medicines are helpful in treating disease or pain, when used correctly. The material at this stage provides a sound basis for work on illegal drugs at the 8–11 age level.

World-wide research has shown that successful drug edcation programmes for young children have four key characteristics:

- The focus of the programme is on the children themselves – their knowledge, feelings, attitudes and decision-making capabilities – rather than on learning about drugs. This is why the classroom strategies provide an excellent starting point for teachers.
- The programme is supported by the whole school, including staff and health professionals. The Action planners can provide the framework for this.
- The programme is supported by and involves parents.
- The programme is co-ordinated with work in the local and wider community.

Keeping Myself Safe

This is included in the Sensitive Issues section because accidents are the most significant cause of death and injury among schoolchildren. While not wanting to restrain children's natural sense of fun and adventure, we do need to develop their 'keeping safe' skills and awareness of possible dangers in the environment.

The research with 4–7 year-olds illustrated the wide range of their fears which spanned monsters, ghosts, aliens, fantasy characters, dangerous and bad adults, dangerous objects and places, traffic and hurt feelings. They believe that the responsibility for keeping safe is not theirs. They believe that among the best ways of keeping safe are to hide, run away, watch TV, stay with mother and lock the doors. This programme has grown out of a fusion of children's perceptions of 'keeping safe' with the messages and skills that we as adults know children must learn, understand and practise. *Health for Life* uses some of these starting points.

- 'Keeping safe' is a sensitive issue in that it can relate to child abuse. Regular opportunities for sharing experiences with teachers and other trusted adults are built into the materials and are clearly signalled. However, teachers will need to follow their school's established policies and procedures in this area.
- Emotional wellbeing is an increasingly important element in teaching children to keep safe and it is highlighted in this section of Health for Life.
- There is considerable emphasis placed on helping children to keep their feelings safe from being hurt.

Me and My Relationships

When children first come to school they are embarking on an important period of physical and mental growth. It is also a period when their interactions with other children and with adults will increase enormously. They have to share the teacher's attention with their classmates and begin to form new networks of friends. These are sometimes single-sex, with girls' groups tending to be smaller. They learn to compare themselves with others, practise their social skills and discover acceptable social behaviour.

As human beings we are characterised by the development of relationships with others. Our lives are continually influenced by the feelings and emotions stimulated by our network of relationships. These start in families and progress to others outside the family as our relationship network grows wider. We cannot escape the effects they have on us because they help to shape the image we have of ourselves. Relationships of all kinds are central to children's lives.

Our research showed that parents, family and friends are very important to young children and so emphasis in the book is placed on friendships, their special people, growing up, and the range of feelings that children experience. This work needs sensitivity. With the involvement of parents and families, children can develop deeper insights, skills and understanding in their dealings with other people. It is important to be especially aware of times of loss or separation that the children experience.

Although not setting out to offer a specific programme of sex education, this work provides a sound basis for more specific sex education starting points in *Health for Life Ages 8–11*.

Conclusion

We are confident that *Health for Life* will enable primary schools to help pupils to develop their knowledge and understanding of PSHE and Citizenship, PSE and PSD topics, and thus fulfil the aim to 'prepare pupils for the opportunities, responsibilities and experiences of adult life.'

Ages 4 and 5

Healthy Lifestyles

Key themes

Key themes: Overview

The overview below offers planned routes for classroom activities that develop key Personal, Social and Health Education and Citizenship skills, drawing on the Action Planners on pages 18, 19 and 20. The Action Planners comprise a series of structured questions that form a spiral curriculum of teaching and learning goals for the 4–5 age range.

Key themes	Content boxes
1 **Growing and changing** • Growing responsibilities and social competencies	**12** → **7** → **8** → **23** (see page 21)
2 **Keeping safe** • Early recognition of dangers and hazards	**10** → **19** → **22** (see page 31)
3 **Medicines and drugs** • Early recognition of the impact of substances	**2** → **3** → **25** (see page 37)

Citizenship and **Emotional Wellbeing** are covered by these key themes.

The content boxes act as starting points for the classroom activities set out in this section. You will find that the questions in each content box stimulate discussion and help you to identify where the children are in their understanding.

It is important that you select and extend the classroom activities according to:

• your PSHE or PSD and Citizenship programmes;
• your Healthy School initiatives.

The additional themes listed below provide further suggestions to develop and extend key health skills. They plot an alternative route through the Action Planners.

Additional themes	Content boxes
1 **Looking at different lifestyles** (including healthy eating, exercise and personal hygiene)	**6** → **16** → **21**
2 **Family life and feelings**	**13** → **14** → **15** → **26**
3 **Reality and fantasy**	**19** → **20**

Me and looking after myself

1

This body of mine: how do I think it looks? What parts can I see? How is it like your body? How is it different from your body and other people's bodies?

2

What goes onto *my* body? Who puts it there? For example soap, water, shampoo, dirt, paint, ointment, plasters, sun, air, clothing, shoes.

3

What goes into *my* body? Who puts it there? For example food, drink, medicines, pills, air, dust, smoke, smells. How does it get in? How does it make me feel? Where do I think it goes?

4

What things can I do when I feel good and healthy? For example run, play, laugh, go out.

5

What can't I do when I am feeling ill or not so healthy? How do I feel? What do I say and do?

What are the words I need to know to talk about:

- the parts of my body, both *my* words and the 'grown-up' words?

- real and pretend?

- size and shape?

- same and different?

- medicines, injections, pills and treatment?

- dangerous and safe?

- growing and growing up?

- asking for help?

- rules?

6

What do I think I do to make and keep myself healthy? My healthy day: what do I do? For example eat, sleep, exercise, play, get fresh air, keep myself clean. What do I think healthy people do or don't do?

7

How do I know I am growing? What can I reach? What can I do now? Which parts of me are growing? What size and shape are people? What size and shape am I? For example small, middle-sized, tall.

8

What do I think made me grow? Who helped me to grow?

9

What do I do (everyday or sometimes) and what do other people do to my body to keep it healthy?

10

What do I think I have to keep safe from? How do I think I do this? What real and pretend things should I keep safe from?

11

What can I do for myself now that I couldn't do before?

Me, my family and my friends

12

Who are the people I meet each day? How do they know I am me? How do they recognise me? How do I recognise them?

17

How do not so healthy people look? What do they do? say? feel? How do I look when I am not so healthy? What do I do? say? feel?

13

Who are my special people? What do I do to make my special people happy? sad? worried? upset? angry?

18

What can I do when I am frightened? lost? bullied? upset? Who can help me?

What are the words I need to know:

- to talk about feelings?
- to describe feeling good, safe and healthy?
- to describe feeling not so good, afraid, worried and lonely?
- to describe being part of different groups?
- to name family and friends?
- to talk about secrets?
- to get people to listen?
- to talk about real and pretend?

14

What makes me feel good? extra good? special? better? Who makes me feel like that? How can I help to take care of the things and places special to me?

19

How do I know which people, places, happenings, friends and pets are real or pretend? Is 'pretend' OK?

15

When do I feel happy or sad? worried? angry? hurt? loving? loved? lost? lonely? How does it feel to have friends? to quarrel? to be left behind? How does it feel when people or pets die?

16

How do healthy people look and feel? How do I look and feel when I am healthy?

20

Good secrets and bad secrets: when should I tell? What do I say? Secret places and happenings: when are they safe? When are they dangerous? How can I say 'No' to people?

Me, my community and my environment

21

Who are the people outside the home, with the special job of keeping me and places healthy and safe? For example doctors, nurses, council workers, safety organisations.

22

Who are the people who keep me safe? What do they do to keep me safe? How do I help them? What do they do to make me feel safe? What makes me feel not so safe? upset? scared?

23

How do the people out there know I'm growing? What new things can I do? How do I recognise the people out there?

24

How do I know I am growing up? What places can I go to on my own? What new things are there to do? What new people are there to recognise? How do I recognise the people out there? What do they say? do? mean? How did the people out there help me grow up? What landmarks do I remember? For example the clinic, the playgroup, swimming.

What are the words I need to know:

- to name the people out there?

- to name places out there?

- to describe the rules out there?

- to describe growing and changing?

- to describe birth and death?

- to describe safe and dangerous?

- to talk about choosing, deciding and saying 'No'?

- to ask for help?

25

Who and what helps me to get better when I'm ill? Where do the people and the medicines come from to make me better? Where do we go to find them? Why must we be careful with medicines?

26

Where do I live? Where do you live? Where do we meet? For example in school, on playgrounds, in shops, on the street, in church, at Sunday school, in other people's homes.

27

Which places around here can we go to? Where are they? Who helps to keep them safe and clean? Which places aren't safe, clean or healthy? What can I do about it?

28

What can I see changing and growing all around here? What is new? old? alive? dead? dying? being born? Where do new things come from? For example babies, plants, pets. Who are the new people in the class? in the home? in the family?

Key theme 1: Growing and changing

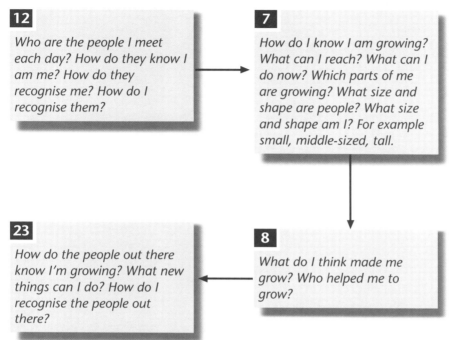

12

Who are the people I meet each day? How do they know I am me? How do they recognise me? How do I recognise them?

7

How do I know I am growing? What can I reach? What can I do now? Which parts of me are growing? What size and shape are people? What size and shape am I? For example small, middle-sized, tall.

23

How do the people out there know I'm growing? What new things can I do? How do I recognise the people out there?

8

What do I think made me grow? Who helped me to grow?

These content boxes are from the Action Planners on pages 18, 19 and 20.

Focus of teaching
- Identifying their own physical growth and change.
- Extending the vocabulary of the human body.
- Recognising and valuing other people's lifestyles, family networks and the rules of interpersonal behaviour.
- Recognising community roles and the interdependence of people.
- Recognising their growing competencies and responsibilities when working as individuals and in groups.

Key skills and competencies
Listening, speaking, discussion; describing people and places; reflecting; comparing; looking for evidence; language of size, shape, body, feelings; individual and shared writing.

Citizenship opportunities
Opportunities for: involving members of the school and the wider community; visits, visitors; strengthening links with home.

Links with children's literature
Stories about characters with different roles in their families.
Stories and poems about other children's lives.
Stories about the world around them.

Growing and changing

Key words

community   home   same   different   describe   recognise   word   picture

Content box 12

12

Who are the people I meet each day? How do they know I am me? How do they recognise me? How do I recognise them?

Activity 1 *Me and the people around me*

■ Talking together. Making a wall story or class book. Drawing, writing and classroom play.

■ Class or group activity, with opportunity for individual work.

Talk with the children about the people they see every day (or most days) at home, at school, and on the way to and from school.

How do the children recognise these people? What do these people do? wear? say? Do they wear special clothes? Where do the children see them? Can they imitate their actions and repeat some of what they hear them do and say?

Draw a large outline of a child. Around the outline write the names of the people the children see and illustrate them (stick people will do).

Ask the children to decide which of these people they see at home, at school, and on the way to and from school.

Invite the children to think about what these people will be doing during the day, while they themselves are at school. In this way the children will start to explore other people's lifestyles and see similarities and differences.

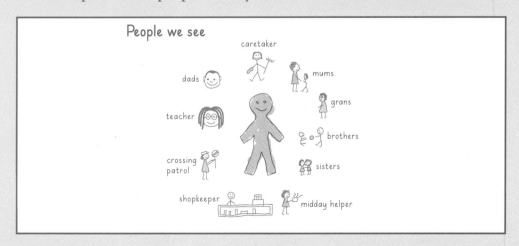

These are the people we have seen today

We all saw
Mr Woods.

Ranjit saw
the postman.

Mrs Smith saw
the caretaker.

Ayesha saw
her gran.

Activity 2 *How do I know I'm me?*

■ Talking together. Drawing and writing.

■ Group and individual activity.

Children delight in trying to explain how people recognise them, and how their friends and families describe them.

Opportunities will arise to talk about:

– names and pet names;

– size;

– shape;

– colour of hair, eyes, skin and clothing.

This could be developed into an individual activity in which children draw themselves and (using the teacher as writer where appropriate) write about how people recognise them.

The children could also describe how specific people might recognise them, for example:

– the crossing patrol;

– the caretaker;

– grandma.

My gran knows it's me.

 Sharon

I go to see her on
Tuesdays.

 Wayne

She sleeps at my
house.

 Lisa

She's known me
since I was a baby.

The crossing patrol knows it's me.

 Jan

I wear
blue wellies.

Glyn

I say hello.

Simon

I don't run.

I always wait.

He's my friend.
He lives near me.

There are **cross-curricular links** with:

– visitors to the classroom;

– visits – to watch some of these people at work;

– stories, poems, rhymes and jingles.

This aspect of lifestyles can be explored and extended in classroom play.

Growing and changing

Key words

growing   growing up   skills   proof   change   evidence   discover   size   shape

Content box 7

> **7**
>
> *How do I know I am growing? What can I reach? What can I do now? Which parts of me are growing? What size and shape are people? What size and shape am I? For example small, middle-sized, tall.*

Activity 1 *How do I know I'm growing?*

■ Talking together. Drawing and writing. Making a wall story and display.

■ Class or group activity, with opportunity for individual work.

Talk with the children about babies. Do the children recall being three years old? two years old? one year old? a baby?

Talk about baby clothes and how small they are. Encourage the children to think about what they could and couldn't do when they were babies.

When I was a baby I couldn't:

walk   talk   climb   get dressed   read

go to school   help my mum   feed myself

When I was a baby I could only:

cry   feed from a bottle   crawl

Make a note of the children's responses. Invite them to sort through a collection of pictures cut from magazines to find pictures of babies, toddlers and school children. Make these into a display.

I am growing I can reach:

the clock   Peter

the shelf   Joss

my coat   Steve

Invite the children to think about how they *know* they are growing. Ask them questions such as 'What are you able to *reach* now?' In what other ways do they know they are growing?

There are **cross-curricular links** with the language of size, for example tall, small, taller, smaller, big, bigger, high, higher, highest, wider, larger.

It might be possible to ask a friend of the school to bring in a baby or toddler to help the children in making comparisons.

Activity 2   *Which parts of me are growing?*

■ Talking together. Drawing and writing. Making a large picture or wall story.

■ Class, small group and individual activity.

Talk with the children about how the different parts of their bodies have grown. How do they know that this growth has happened? Write down and display the children's ideas and illustrate them, or ask them to contribute to the illustrations.

Read and reread the display with the children. Encourage them to make individual versions to take away and add to at home.

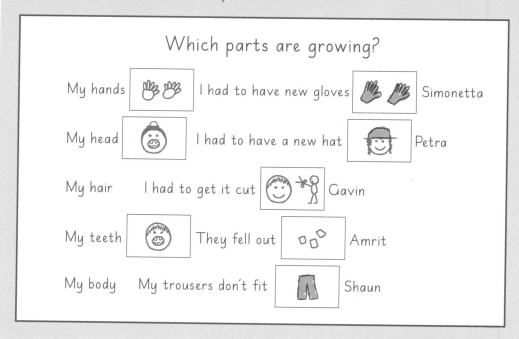

Which parts are growing?

My hands   I had to have new gloves   Simonetta

My head   I had to have a new hat   Petra

My hair   I had to get it cut   Gavin

My teeth   They fell out   Amrit

My body   My trousers don't fit   Shaun

Activity 3 *What size and shape am I?*

- Talking together. Drawing and painting.

- Class, group and individual activity.

Talk with the children about the different sizes and shapes of people (you will need to be sensitive to children's feelings about their own size and shape).

Extend their language of size and shape: tall, small, middle-sized, big, bigger, biggest, thin, not so thin, long legs, long arms.

Ask the children to draw or paint pictures of different people, pets, flowers and trees on the theme ... can be all shapes and sizes'. Label them with the appropriate vocabulary.

People can be all shapes and sizes.

tall　　　middle size　　　small

Flowers and trees　　　dogs and cats

can be all shapes and sizes.

There are **cross-curricular links** with:

- PE – size and shape can be explored in physical activities such as reaching and stretching up;

- mathematical language – sorting and grouping activities can be introduced or reinforced;

- science – skills such as observation can be introduced.

Growing and changing

remember	family	community	food	love

Content box 8

> **8**
>
> *What do I think made me grow? Who helped me to grow?*

Activity 1 *What made me grow? Who helped me to grow?*

- Talking together. Drawing and writing. Making a display.

- Class or group activity, with opportunity for individual work.

Talk with the children about how much they have grown. Invite them to draw and label pictures of people and all the things that helped them to grow. (You can write for them.)

Look at the children's responses and make a note of the most frequent, the most unusual and the most unexpected responses.

Use the children's responses to make up a large shared picture. Make up a rhyme or jingle to read and reread as a piece of shared writing.

What made me grow?

baby food   lots of sleep   lots of dinner   going out in   they loved me
my pram

Who helped me grow?

my gran and   my brother and   the doctor and nurse and
my mum   our dog   the man in the shop

There are **cross-curricular links** with literacy, stories, poems, rhymes and songs.

Use the theme of growth as the starting point for portrait painting and picture-making.

Growing and changing

Content box 23

> **23**
>
> *How do the people out there know I'm growing? What new things can I do? How do I recognise the people out there?*

Activity 1   *Now I am growing – where do I go?*

■ Talking together. Classroom play. Drawing and writing.

■ Group or pair activity, with opportunity for individual work.

Talk with the children about some of the places they go to now they are growing up. (This is an opportunity for some relevant safety education.) Who takes them? Do they ever go alone? Do they *want* to go? Do they *have* to go? You could plan to visit some of these places.

Use classroom play to encourage the children to explore what happens when they go to these places. What do people say at these places? Do these places have a special vocabulary of their own?

Invite the children to write about both the classroom play and the visits they make.

We have been playing going to the library.

Joanie was the library lady.

    She said

Take care of the books.

Philo stamped the books.

Sonia put the books away.

Activity 2 *Now I am growing up, what can I do?*

I can clean my own teeth.

I can choose my drink.

I can read a book.

I can put my shoes and coat on.

I can be responsible.

■ Talking together. Drawing and writing. Sorting and grouping pictures.

■ Class, group and individual activity.

Talk with the children about the things they can now do for themselves. Ask them to draw and write about the things they can do and be responsible for doing.

Provide the children with a collection of pictures cut from magazines. Include pictures of people of all ages, from a variety of lifestyles, doing a variety of activities. Ask the children to sort these into sets, using the criteria:

– things I can do *now*;

– things I will be able to do *soon*;

– things I can't do *yet*;

– things I want to do;

– things I need to practise.

Ask the children to talk you through their sorting procedure. Talk about the things they want to be able to do. Can they start to learn some of the skills (or see the risks) involved?

There are **cross-curricular links** with:

– classroom play;

– visits and visitors;

– stories, poems and rhymes;

– art.

Reflection and action

Look back with the children at all they have learned about their roles in being and staying healthy, shared with the significant people around them.

• Remind them of their progress in the skills of working together and recognising their responsibilities.

• Ask them to practise these skills and to look for other people in the community who help them grow and grow up.

Key theme 2: Keeping safe

10

What do I think I have to keep safe from? How do I think I do this? What real and pretend things should I keep safe from?

19

How do I know which people, places, happenings, friends and pets are real or pretend? Is 'pretend' OK?

22

Who are the people who keep me safe? What do they do to keep me safe? How do I help them? What do they do to make me feel safe? What makes me feel not so safe? upset? scared?

These content boxes are from the Action Planners on pages 18, 19 and 20.

Focus of teaching
- Recognising hazards and dangers in their changing environment.
- Recognising and keeping the rules of being and staying safe in all relevant situations.
- Recognising that they are growing into greater independence and will need a greater range of skills.
- Recognising that there are people in the community who are charged with keeping children safe, but this requires children to co-operate and take on some responsibilities.
- Knowing who to tell and how to tell when they feel uncertain, threatened, bullied or abused, physically or emotionally.

Key skills and competencies
Listening, speaking, discussion; recognising differences in situations; growing understanding of risks; decision making; making people listen; retelling experiences in sequence; extending the language of emotions; class and group skills.

Citizenship opportunities
Opportunities for: involving families and the community; visits to see people at work in the community, reinforced through role-play.

Links with children's literature
Stories where characters recognise or fail to recognise dangers ahead. Stories where children share their concerns and feelings with understanding adults.

Keeping safe

Key words

safe   dangerous   home   school   rules   practise   responsible   bully

Content box 10

> **10**
>
> *What do I think I have to keep safe from? How do I think I do this? What real and pretend things should I keep safe from?*

Activity 1 *What do I think I have to keep safe from?*

■ Talking together. Drawing and writing.

■ Class or group activity, with opportunity for individual work.

Explore the children's perceptions of what they think they have to keep safe from by inviting them to draw pictures of themselves keeping safe, and pictures of things they are keeping safe from. Invite the children to share what they have drawn. Help them to label their drawings, particularly what they see as hazards and dangers and why.

Talk with the children about the real and imaginary hazards which are found indoors and outdoors.

Display some of their drawings and dictated writing.

This is our class keeping ourselves safe

Encourage the children to talk about how they keep themselves safe from the hazards they have identified. Their answers are likely to focus on 'don'ts', for example 'Don't touch', 'Don't go out', 'Don't let them in', 'Don't run'; or, 'Hide', 'Run away', 'Hold on', 'Go and watch TV'. Encourage them to extend these ideas by talking about the importance of:

- staying with the known;

- not wandering off or going off with older children or people they don't know;

- not touching or tasting;

- knowing how to say 'No', 'Please help me';

- telling a safe adult;

- learning that different places have different rules.

Ask the children to practise 'telling': describing places, people and feelings.

Cross-curricular links: classroom play, movement, drama and PE can all be used to reinforce these themes.

Keeping safe

Key words

real   imagine   pretend   cartoons   advertisements   persuade   choose

Content box 19

19

How do I know which people, places, happenings, friends and pets are real or pretend? Is 'pretend' OK?

Activity 1 *Real and pretend people, places and happenings*

- Sharing literature and television programmes. Drawing and writing. Making a wall story.

- Class and group activity, with opportunity for individual work.

Literature can provide a starting point for children to talk about real or imaginary characters and happenings; about toys which sometimes have a life of their own; about imaginary friends and pets. Television programmes will also provide a starting point for discussion.

Invite the children to draw and label some of the real and imaginary characters and happenings they have encountered.

Collect their observations, illustrations and writing, and make a wall story for reading, rereading and adding to. It could be interesting and useful to invite members of the children's families to come and share the wall story.

Without discouraging children from having imaginary worlds, it is important for their safety that they learn to differentiate between reality and fantasy. You will need to take into account the impact of television on children, as by its very nature it makes it difficult for them to distinguish between what is real and what is fantasy.

Keeping safe

Content box 22

> **22**
>
> *Who are the people who keep me safe? What do they do to keep me safe? How do I help them? What do they do to make me feel safe? What makes me feel not so safe? upset? scared?*

Activity 1 *The people who keep me safe*

- Talking together. Classroom play. Painting and writing. Making a wall story.
- Group and class activity, with opportunity for shared and individual work.

Invite the children to think about all the people who help to keep them safe throughout the day. Explore this in movement and classroom play: work through the children's day, starting with getting up in the morning.

Briefly illustrate the list of people (stick people will do) and places which are part of the children's day, for example:

- in my house;
- on the way to school;
- at school;
- out of school;
- my family;

- crossing patrol;
- teacher, caretaker, school nurse;
- other adults: friends, religious figures, police officers, park and pool attendants, fire brigade, ambulance people.

Ask the children to paint large pictures of the people who help to keep them safe. Help the children to label the pictures, then make a wall story.

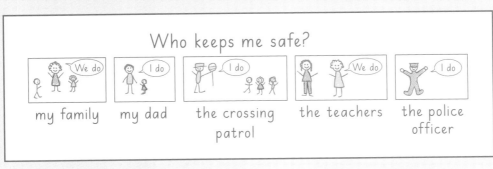

Activity 2 *What do I do to help?*

- Talking together. Drawing and writing.

- Class or group activity.

Reread with the children the wall story they made in Activity 1: 'Who keeps me safe?'.

Look at each character in turn. Invite the children to say or act out ways in which they could make the characters happy by helping them, and ways in which they might make the characters sad, worried or angry by not helping them.

Follow up this activity by inviting the children to draw themselves being helpful (or not so helpful) with labels or explanations.

Activity 3 *How do they make me feel safe?*

- Talking together. Classroom play and role-play. Stories.

- Small group activity, with opportunity for family work.

Talk with the children about what these helpful people do or say to make people feel safe. Young children are often very aware of this aspect of safety and can be encouraged to put their thoughts into words. Classroom play often provides the key.

! This could be the time to introduce small group talk about people who do not make us feel safe, such as bullies, people who tease, people who push smaller people about or people who touch our bodies in ways which upset or threaten us. If classroom play and role-play have been well established then this could be a good time to explore and practise the skills of moving away, of telling an adult and of saying 'No'. **!**

This is a good time to use stories about conquering or reducing fear, dealing with threats and with real and imaginary fears and dangers.

You can involve visits or visitors and invite family co-operation and reinforcement.

Family work: you could ask parents to encourage the children to explain what they have been doing in school when they take home their drawing and writing.

Reflection and action

Look back with the children at all they have learned about keeping their bodies and feelings safe.
- Remind them that they have an important role to play and make the adults' jobs easier by the way they themselves behave.
- Remind them to practise their skills for keeping safe, and the rules inside and outside school.

Key theme 3: Medicines and drugs

2

What goes onto my body?
Who puts it there?
For example soap, water,
shampoo, dirt, paint,
ointment, plasters, sun, air,
clothing, shoes

3

What goes into my body?
Who puts it there? For
example food, drink,
medicines, pills, air, dust,
smoke, smells. How does it get
in? How does it make me feel?
Where do I think it goes?

25

Who and what helps me to
get better when I'm ill? Where
do the people and the
medicines come from to make
me better? Where do we go to
find them? Why must we be
careful with medicines?

These content boxes are from the Action Planners on pages 18, 19 and 20.

Focus of teaching
- Heightened awareness of what goes onto and into their bodies, the source of this and their own role in this.
- Understanding and working with children's views of their body systems and where substances go.
- Extending understanding that all medicines are drugs but not all drugs are medicines and that medicines, pills, injections, alcohol and nicotine are dangerous.
- Extending understanding of the rules of using medicines to prevent, recover from or control a health problem.
- Understanding that we all have a right of access to health care but also have responsibilities for staying healthy.

Key skills and competencies
Listening, speaking, discussion; recognising that actions have outcomes; stopping and thinking before acting; recognising rules; extending the language of risk and decision making; writing and sharing.

Citizenship opportunities
Opportunities for: visits from school nurse and pharmacist; visits to surgeries and clinics, reinforced through role-play.

Links with children's literature
Stories where characters deal with situations in different ways.
Stories about being ill and getting better.
Stories where characters eat too much of something.

Medicines and drugs

Key words

aware   come from   go to   feel   dangerous   choose   decide   persuade

Content box 2

2

*What goes onto my body?
Who puts it there?
For example soap, water,
shampoo, dirt, paint,
ointment, plasters, sun, air,
clothing, shoes*

Activity 1 *What goes onto my body?*

■ Talking together. Drawing and writing. Making a wall story.

■ Class or group activity.

Ask the children what they put onto their bodies when they get up in the morning. Their first responses may focus on clothing, so invite them to think of other situations, for example getting washed.

Encourage the children to talk about other times of the day. What else do they put onto their bodies when they are out playing? when they are having their hair washed? when they have a sore or a cut?

Draw a large outline of a child. Around the outline draw or stick on pictures of the things children think go onto their bodies, and label them. Both you and the children can do the drawing and writing as you talk. Read through the work as you go. Read and reread the wall story.

What goes onto our bodies?

Talk with the children about how they feel when they (or someone else) puts these different things onto their bodies. Which of these things feel good, and which feel not so good? Which of these things please adults, and which make adults cross? Why?

Ask the children to pick out any of these situations which might be dangerous and encourage them to say why. (It is important to discover the children's explanations before you talk with them about sensitive issues.)

Activity 2 *Who puts it there?*

- Talking together.
- Class or small group activity, with opportunity for family work.

Return to the wall story in Activity 1: 'What goes onto our bodies?'.

Reread the captions with the children, each time asking: 'Who puts it there?' The children will have differing and interesting answers, especially relating to air, dust and sun. In each case ask them to explain: 'What happens to it?' 'Does it disappear?' 'Does someone take it off? If so, who?' 'Did *you* decide to put it onto your body?' 'Did someone else tell you to put it onto your body?' 'Did someone persuade you to do it?'. This would be a good opportunity to practise saying 'No, I won't', 'I'll ask someone', and walking away.

Family work: some children could make their own versions of the wall story. The children could take these home and explain them to their families and invite them to make additions.

Medicines and drugs

Key words

aware   inside   appear   disappear   feelings   sniff   taste   choose   persuade

Content box 3

> **3**
>
> *What goes into my body? Who puts it there? For example food, drink, medicines, pills, air, dust, smoke, smells. How does it get in? How does it make me feel? Where do I think it goes?*

Activity 1 *What goes into my body?*

- Talking together. Recording views.

- Classroom and individual activities.

The strategies and activities suggested for Content box 2: 'What goes *onto* my body?' can be used again, but with a change of focus.

Encourage children to think of all the ways in which 'things' can enter their bodies. For example: by breathing, eating, drinking and sniffing; via mouth, ears and eyes; by injection or by accident (splinters, wasp stings, nails, pins or thorns). Encourage them to think widely, to include medicines, pills, berries, smoke, fumes, pleasant smells and scents. Remind them of the dangers of things they cannot identify or could mistake for sweets.

Talk with the children about their feelings when different things enter their bodies, such as delight, pain or fear. Invite them to talk about who puts these things into them and to identify those things which are dangerous, those which they should only do with adult permission and supervision, and those which they should never do. Encourage them to explain why they believe certain things could be dangerous and what the outcomes might be. It may be possible at this stage to talk about dirt and germs getting into their bodies and the importance of personal hygiene. It is important not to illustrate germs as large, ferocious beings, but to remind the children that germs are invisible.

It is important at this stage to discover as much as possible about the children's perceptions of what is inside their bodies, before planning any teaching about the dangers of specific substances on different parts of the body and body systems.

Activity 2 *Where do I think it all goes?*

■ Painting and drawing. Making a display. Talking together.

■ Individual or small group activity.

Invite the children to paint large-scale pictures of what they think is inside their bodies. Display the pictures and talk with the children about what happens when all the different things they have talked about enter their bodies. Where does food and drink go? pills? injections? The children's unprompted perceptions of the bloodstream and digestion will be most revealing.

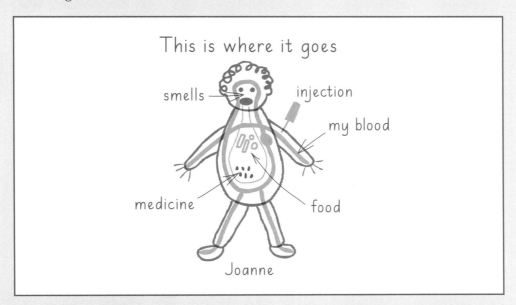

This is where it goes

smells — injection

my blood

medicine food

Joanne

Most children will not be ready for formal descriptions, diagrams and language for parts of the body. The analysis of their perceptions and explanations will enable you to plan your teaching more effectively and to monitor changes in their understanding.

Without attempting to explain body systems, it is possible to explain that what we eat, drink, sniff or are injected with finds its way all round our bodies. Explain that it does not, as many young children think, go into part of the body and stay there.

Medicines and drugs

Content box 25

> **25**
>
> *Who and what helps me to get better when I'm ill? Where do the people and the medicines come from to make me better? Where do we go to find them? Why must we be careful with medicines?*

Activity 1 *Who helps me to get better when I'm ill?*

- Talking together and using mime and classroom play. Making a wall story or class book. Drawing and painting.

- Class, group and individual activity.

Invite the children to share what it is like to be ill through talk, mime and classroom play. How did they look? What hurt? What itched? What did they have to do or not do? Did they have to take any medicine? With the children, note down their responses as a piece of shared writing.

When I was ill:

I cried.

I was sick.

The doctor came.

I stayed in bed.

I was brave and took my medicine.

I itched all over.

Invite the children to write their own accounts of what it is like to be ill and to illustrate them. Display these around the shared writing as a wall story.

Activity 2 *Where did the people come from to make me better?*

- Talking together.

- Class or group activity.

Reread the wall story from Activity 1.

Ask the children who and what makes them better. Write down their responses, read and then reread them.

Can the children say where all these people and things came from? Ask them to write about and illustrate this.

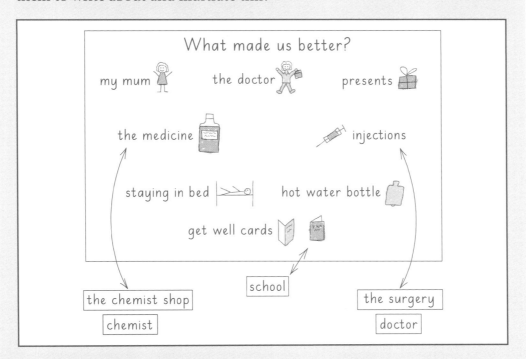

There are opportunities here to talk about the caring aspect of getting better, as well as to look at where medicines and pills come from. With the children's help, build up some simple rules:

– only take medicines when they are given to you by a doctor, nurse, parent or responsible adult;

– do not taste, try or touch anything you find in bottles, jars or packs of pills;

– do not pick up needles or anything which looks sharp.

Activity 3 *Keeping safe with medicines*

- Making a collage. Talking together. Role-play.

- Class or small group activity, with opportunity for family work.

Give the children pictures cut from magazines depicting toothpaste, talc, soap, shampoo, cough medicine, tablets, creams and lotions.

Stick these pictures onto an outline of an open cupboard with several shelves.

Invite the children to talk about the items and to identify and label those which are dangerous. Ask them to explain why. (This will enable you to see something of the logic they use and to gauge the impact of the previous activities on safety.)

Encourage the children to use the collage as a backdrop for a small-scale play, using improvised paper figures or dolls. Help them to devise role-plays with good and not so good endings.

Family work: children could take home an individual version of this work to share with their families.

We have been learning about medicines and pills and keeping safe.

We made a picture of a cupboard with lots of things in.

We put ● by the dangerous ones.

Can we look in our cupboard and see if there are any dangerous things?

These are the dangerous things in our cupboard:

bleach

aspirin

There are **cross-curricular links** with visits to and from people in the community.

Reflection and action

Look back with the children at all they have learned about medicines and other substances.
- Remind them of the rules they have helped to identify and their progress in keeping these rules.
- Ask them to put their learning into practice, especially when there are younger children around.
- Remind them that adults or other children might try to persuade them to try or taste something. Revise what to do in such situations.
- Remind them that 'telling an adult' is a good strategy and is not 'telling tales'.

Ages 4 and 5

Sensitive Issues

Key themes

Key theme 1:
The world of drugs

The six content boxes on page 47 each have a distinctive focus and act as starting points for the classroom activities. The questions in each content box stimulate discussion and help you to build on previous skills and knowledge and to identify where the children are in their understanding.

It is important that you select and extend the classroom activities according to: your PSHE or PSD and Citizenship programmes; your Healthy School initiatives; the school's Drug Education Policy; and involve the support of the children's families, the school governors and the local community.

Focus of teaching
- Recognising that substances (whatever we put onto or into our bodies) affect our bodies.
- Extending the language of the body and body systems.
- Understanding that some people need medicines at different times to help prevent or cure illnesses, and that some people may need medicines all the time in order to stay healthy.
- Wider understanding of the importance of the safe handling of medicines, and their role in this.
- Recognising they have a role in the 'getting better' process.
- Early recognition of pressure, especially to try (touch, taste, sniff or puff) substances, and how to deal with this.
- Reinforcing understanding that all medicines are drugs but not all drugs are medicines.

Key skills and competencies
Class and group discussion; language of feelings and relationships; categorising and ranking views; rule making; shared presentation of work; recognising differences.

Citizenship opportunities
Opportunities for: behaving as a responsible citizen; exploring the world of medical care; visits to and from community organisations; work with local Drug Action teams; extending to Governors and parents what is appropriate early drug education.

Links with children's literature
Stories, fables and poems where characters recognise someone is using persuasion to get their own way.

The world of drugs

1

What goes onto my body?
How and when does it get there? Who tells me to put it onto my body? What is it for? Which part of my body does it go onto? Do I think it's safe? How does it feel? Do I like it? How do I react? Does it hurt? Should I ask someone about it? Who do I tell? Who can I trust? What do I say?

2

What goes into my body?
How does it get in? Who puts it there? Why? Who tells me to put it there? Does it get there on purpose or by accident? How does it feel? taste? look? smell? Do I like it? What do I do if I don't like it, or if it hurts, or if it worries me? What can I say?

3

What is inside my body?
What is under my skin? Where do things go once they get inside me? What happens to them?

4

Who needs medicines?
When have I had to take medicines? Why? Was I ill? Who told me to take the medicine? Was it a safe person? Where did we get the medicine? Was it a safe place? Where did we keep it? Was it a safe place? Who gave it to me? Was it a safe person? What did it taste like and look like? What did I say? How did I feel at first? How did I feel after a while?

5

What's in here?
Where might medicines and other dangerous things be found? What's under here? What's it for? Who put it there? Do I know what it is? Who does it belong to? Is this a dangerous place to look? What can I say if someone tries to make me touch or taste it? What can I do? Who can I tell? How do I tell them?

6

How do I feel when I am ill?
How do I look? What do I do? What do I say? What do I ask for? What helps to make me better? Who helps me to get better? What do I do to help?

Key messages
for learning to live in a drug-using world

Learn:

- what goes onto and into your body;

- when to say 'No' and 'Stop';

- when to ask for help;

- about medicines, pills and injections;

- about the places where you might find
things which aren't safe to touch, taste or sniff;

- about the everyday things which can harm you, for example
tobacco, smoke, sprays, liquids and some drinks;

- about your feelings and which feelings you can trust;

- who you can trust and confide in;

- to tell people how you feel;

- to share these messages.

Understand:

- that some people need medicines at different times to
help them get better or to stop them being ill;

- that you can help yourself feel better and get better;

- that all medicines are drugs but not all drugs are medicines.

Practise:

- telling people how you feel;

- finding someone you trust to talk to if something
or someone is worrying you.

Share these key messages with parents, families and people in the community so that they can support and reinforce them.

The world of drugs

Key words

body   head   arms   legs   sure   not sure   worried   feelings   persuade

Content box 1

1

*What goes onto my body?
How and when does it get
there? Who tells me to put it
onto my body? What is it for?
Which part of my body does it
go onto? Do I think it's safe?
How does it feel? Do I like it?
How do I react? Does it hurt?
Should I ask someone about
it? Who do I tell? Who can I
trust? What do I say?*

Activity 1 *What goes onto my body?*

■ Talking together. Making a wall story. Drawing and collecting pictures.
Categorising.

■ Class or group activity.

Draw a large outline of a child. Write the children's responses to these
questions around the outline: 'What goes onto my body?' 'Which part of
my body do they touch?'

Invite the children to give you their own drawings and pictures cut from
magazines which can be added to the larger picture.

What goes onto my body?

insects   clothes
shampoo   head   plasters
dust   ointment
dirt   arm   body
kisses   cobwebs
glue   leg   foot   lotion
paint
fire   rain
things you   sun
don't know

Ask the children to categorise
(using colour coding) those items
which they see in these terms:

– OK;

– I'm not sure. I'll ask someone
about it;

– It's not OK – so I
won't let it touch
my body.

Practise with the
children: Say 'No'!

Stop!
Think!

Remind them of all the people around them who will listen
and help.

Explore with the children who put these different items onto their bodies. This will involve looking for different categories.

Introduce this question to the children: 'If someone tried to persuade you to put something onto your body, what would you do? What would you say? Who would you tell?'

Help them to practise saying: 'No, I won't', 'I'll ask someone', 'It's dangerous'.

Activity 2 *How does it feel?*

■ Talking together. Making a wall chart. Writing and drawing.

■ Class or group activity, with opportunity for individual work.

Invite the children to think about how they react to things which touch their bodies. Do they like these feelings or not? What do they do? Make a note of their responses, display them as a wall chart and talk with the children about them. Alternatively, you could ask the children to work individually, write about and illustrate their reactions and then share this work with you and their classmates.

I rub it in.

It feels warm.

It stings my eyes.

It tickles.

It smells horrid.

It makes me feel better.

It scares me.

It helps my asthma.

Explore with the children how they would react if an unknown substance touched their bodies, for example a liquid, a powder or an ointment. How would they deal with this? Who might they tell at home, at school or outside school? Encourage them to practise coping with this situation.

The world of drugs

Key words

nose   mouth   skin   sniff   wheeze   persuade   dare   injection

Content box 2

> **2**
>
> *What goes into my body?*
> *How does it get in? Who puts*
> *it there? Why? Who tells me to*
> *put it there? Does it get there*
> *on purpose or by accident?*
> *How does it feel? taste? look?*
> *smell? Do I like it? What do I*
> *do if I don't like it, or if it*
> *hurts, or if it worries me?*
> *What can I say?*

Activity 1 *What goes into my body?*

- Talking together. Making a wall story. Drawing and collecting pictures. Categorising.

- Class or group activity.

Invite the children to make a wall story, similar to the one made for Content box 1, in order to explore 'What goes *into* my body?' Encourage them to include food, drink, dust, cigarette smoke, fresh air, sun, sprays, medicines, pills, injections, thorns, splinters, foreign bodies and unknown things. Write the children's responses around the outline.

Invite the children to talk about and illustrate the questions: 'How does it get in?' and 'Who told me to do it?'

Encourage the children to categorise their answers to the question: 'How does it get in?' Categories might include:

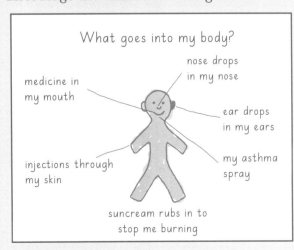

What goes into my body?

nose drops in my nose

medicine in my mouth

ear drops in my ears

my asthma spray

injections through my skin

suncream rubs in to stop me burning

– I did it;

– the doctor or the nurse did it;

– by accident;

– on purpose;

– someone told me to;

– someone dared me to.

Remind the children of how to refuse to take part in dares.

51

Activity 2 *How does it feel?*

- Talking together. Drawing and writing.

- Class or group activity, with opportunity for individual work.

Talk with the children about the ways in which they reacted to things entering their bodies.

Did they:

- ask or tell someone whether it was safe?

- swallow?

- sniff?

- like it?

- cry?

- sneeze?

- say 'Don't'?

- stop wheezing?

- feel better?

This would be a good opportunity to talk about children who are asthmatic, diabetic or have other problems, and how the class can help them.

Invite the children to illustrate themselves reacting to some of these situations. Add speech bubbles to their pictures in which they can write (or you could write for them) what they said or felt.

Cross-curricular links: you could explore this theme further using language work in a similar way to the activities for Content box 1.

The world of drugs

Content box 3

> **3**
>
> **What is inside my body?**
> What is under my skin? Where
> do things go once they get
> inside me? What happens to
> them?

Activity 1 *What is inside my body?*

- ■ Painting and drawing. Talking together.

- ■ Class or group activity.

Ask the children to paint or draw large-scale pictures of themselves which
show what they think is under their skin. Talk with them about what they
have drawn and how they think their body systems work.

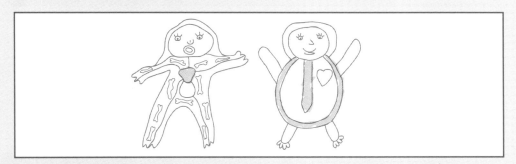

It is particularly interesting to look at the children's paintings to discover if,
and how, they draw the blood circulation system. Does it appear as a single
continuous line around the outside of the body? At this stage it is more
important to focus on the children's own explanations and drawings, looking
closely at what they put in or leave out, rather than to offer them correct
diagrams.

Remind the children of the activity in which you all talked about things which
entered the body. Ask them to explain or illustrate what they think happens to
these things inside their bodies. What do they do? Where do they go?

The children's explanations and the specific words they use could provide
you with valuable insights and starting points for offering them new and
appropriate information.

You could repeat this activity later in the year as an evaluation of the
children's increased understanding of their body systems.

The world of drugs

Key words

medicine   spray   ill   doctor   prescription   chemist   cupboard   rules
dangerous   safe person

Content box 4

4

Who needs medicines?
*When have I had to take
medicines? Why? Was I ill?
Who told me to take the
medicine? Was it a safe
person? Where did we get the
medicine? Was it a safe place?
Where did we keep it? Was it a
safe place? Who gave it to
me? Was it a safe person?
What did it taste like and look
like? What did I say? How did
I feel at first? How did I feel
after a while?*

Activity 1 *When have I had to take medicines?*

- ■ Talking together. Drawing and writing.

- ■ Class or group activity.

Invite the children to talk about when and why they have needed
medicines in the past. Ask them to draw pictures which illustrate one
such occasion, and to add some writing (or dictated writing) to their
picture.

Remind the children that all medicines can be dangerous.

Ask the children to share their pictures. Talk with them about their
experiences, such as:

– going to the doctor;

– going to hospital;

– going abroad;

– having a temperature;

– having an asthma attack.

Where appropriate, include examples of children who take medicine
regularly or who have some medication always on hand, for example
children with asthma.

Activity 2 *Where did the medicines come from?*

■ Talking together. Drawing. Collecting pictures. Writing.

■ Class or group activity, with opportunity for individual work and family work.

Explore with the children how medicines look and how they are taken. Ask them to illustrate their responses with their own drawings or using pictures from magazines. Look again at what they said and how they felt and reacted when they had to take medicines.

Talk about, and ask the children to illustrate and label, their responses to the following questions:

– Who gave them the medicines? (For example my mum, the doctor, the nurse.)

– Was this a safe person?

– Where did they come from? (For example the bathroom cupboard, the chemist, my gran's handbag, the shelf in the kitchen, the clinic.)

– Are these safe places to keep medicines? You could colour code the children's illustrations to denote which of them represent safe or unsafe situations.

– How did they feel at first when they took the medicine? How did they feel later on?

These activities provide the opportunity to introduce the following 'medicine wise' rules:

– all medicines have drugs in them and this makes them dangerous;

– only take medicines if they are given to you by a safe person;

– never take anyone else's medicine;

– never touch, taste or take anything just because someone tells you to. Say 'No, I won't', 'I'll ask' or 'I'll tell someone'.

Talk through these rules with the children and help them to learn and practise them.

Family work: the children could take copies of the 'medicine wise' rules to explain to their families.

There are **cross-curricular links** with topics which focus on the community and people who help.

The world of drugs

Content box 5

> **5**
>
> *What's in here?*
> *Where might medicines and other dangerous things be found? What's under here? What's it for? Who put it there? Do I know what it is? Who does it belong to? Is this a dangerous place to look? What can I say if someone tries to make me touch or taste it? What can I do? Who can I tell? How do I tell them?*

Activity 1 *Where are medicines found?*

- Talking together. Collecting pictures, drawing and writing.

- Class or group activity.

Talk with the children about the places in and around the home where people put medicines or other dangerous substances. What things might they find:

- on windowsills?

- in bathroom cupboards or on shelves by the side of the bath?

- on bedside tables, shelves or cabinets?

- in handbags, cupboards, first aid boxes, pockets and glove compartments in cars?

- in garden sheds, garages, storage places and under sinks?

and which of these things could contain chemicals of some kind?

What's in here?

on the windowsill   on the table   in the shed

Invite the children to collect or draw pictures of the many things which might be found in these places, and to label them. Add to their responses everyday items such as sweets, medicines, pills, cigarettes, matches, different kinds of drinks (including alcohol), bottles, jars and containers of different kinds, garden and garage materials, sprays, glue, powders, animal food and medication.

Invite the children to explore and categorise these places and items, by answering questions such as:

– who left it there?

– what is it for?

– is it safe to look in here?

– is it safe to touch, pick up, taste or try this?

– what must I do if I see or find this?

Encourage the children to ask of each place and item: 'Is this safe?' 'Should I be careful?' 'Am I sure?' 'Should I touch?' 'Should I ask for help?' 'Should I tell someone?'

Again you could use a simple colour-coding system on their pictures to show what is safe and unsafe.

Activity 2 *What do I say if someone tries to persuade me?*

■ Talking together. Making a wall story or class/individual books. Classroom play.

■ Class or group activity, with opportunity for individual work and family work.

Here it is possible to reinforce the strategies for dealing with persuasion. Ask the children what they think they would say or do if someone tried to pressurise them into touching or tasting something which might not be safe. Help them to practise ways of saying: 'No, I won't', 'It's dangerous', 'I'll ask someone'.

The children's work on Content box 5 could be brought together to make a wall story, class book or individual books which the children could take home to share with their **families**.

Many of these situations could be explored further using classroom play as a good way to rehearse coping strategies.

The world of drugs

Content box 6

> **6**
>
> **How do I feel when I am ill?**
> How do I look? What do I do? What do I say? What do I ask for? What helps to make me better? Who helps me to get better? What do I do to help?

Activity 1   *How do I feel when I am ill?*

■ Painting and drawing. Talking together. Writing.

■ Class or group activity, with opportunity for individual work.

Invite the children to paint or draw pictures of themselves feeling ill and to display them.

Talk with the children about how they look and feel, and what they can or cannot do when they are ill. Make a note of their responses, particularly the language they use to express their feelings. Invite them to use this language by adding it to their pictures and explaining how they feel.

Activity 2   *What helps to make me better?*

■ Talking together. Painting and drawing.

■ Class or group activity.

Explore with the children what they think makes them feel better. What do they ask for apart from medication? For example love, company and rest. Who provides this? Talk about these people. What do they do, say and feel? Again, make a note of the children's language.

It is important to end by looking at what the children think they did to help themselves get well. Emphasise that this is an important part of growing up.

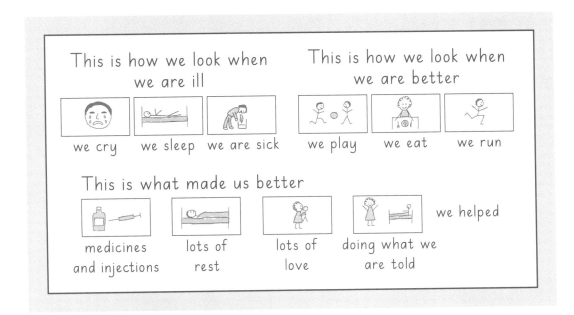

This is how we look when we are ill

we cry   we sleep   we are sick

This is how we look when we are better

we play   we eat   we run

This is what made us better

medicines and injections   lots of rest   lots of love   doing what we are told   we helped

Reflection and action

Look back with the children at all they have learned about the world of medicines, drugs and other substances.

- Remind them of the rules about medicines which can make us better but which need to be used safely. Remind them of their roles in this.
- Remind them to share what they have learned with people at school, and to practise keeping these rules both at home and in school.

Key theme 2:
Keeping myself safe

The five content boxes on page 61 each have a distinctive focus and act as starting points for the classroom activities. The questions in each content box stimulate discussion and help you to build on previous skills and knowledge and to identify where the children are in their understanding.

It is important that you select and extend the classroom activities according to: your PSHE or PSD and Citizenship programmes; your Healthy School initiatives: Health and Safety regulations; child abuse procedures.

Focus of teaching
- Understanding that they need to keep their feelings as well as their bodies safe from being harmed.
- Difference between real, imaginary and pretend people and places.
- Widening strategies for keeping safe in a range of situations.
- Difference between safe, risky and dangerous.
- Recognising different kinds of secrets: 'fun' secrets, threatening secrets.
- Knowing who they are, their personal details and who is in charge of them.
- Widening understanding of hazards and dangers both in and out of class.
- Recognising that their feelings can affect how they behave, particularly in potentially hazardous situations.
- Understanding that there are people, rules and laws to keep them safe in their lives, who these people are and what they do.
- Recognising that they themselves contribute to being and keeping safe.

Key skills and competencies
Valuing self and others as unique but also members of different networks; listening, speaking, discussion; describing people, places, situations; retelling in sequence; naming degrees of dangers; language of places, distance, relationships; language of feelings and emotions.

Citizenship opportunities
Opportunities for visits from: Railway Safety Officers; Environmental Health Officers; Home / Road Safety Officers; Police / Fire / Ambulance Services; others who emphasise that prevention can be the children's role too. Opportunities to: look at rules around school for children, adults and visitors; review why there is a security system; look at local by-laws, laws of the country.

Links with children's literature
Stories where: characters go out into the world and recognise and cope with dangers (by their own skills, not by magic); the children can see that being saved by magic happens in literature but not in real life; characters need help, make efforts to find it.

Keeping myself safe

1
Focus on feelings
What do I think I have to keep safe from? How do I think I keep safe? What is real and what is pretend? Which threats, promises and secrets are real and which are pretend? Do I always have to keep secrets? Which secrets are good and which are bad? Who can I ask for help? If I tell someone will I get into trouble?
When am I most at risk?

2
Focus on me
Who am I? Where am I? Where have I been? Who is (was) with me? Who is in charge of me? Where do I live? Who is there? How can I get there safely? What should I do when I am lost? What should I do to get help? What should I not do? How can I ask for help?
When am I most at risk?

3
Focus on indoors
What is good about my home? Am I warm, fed and happy? Why must I be careful with fires, cookers, electricity, gas, television, stairs and medicines? How do accidents happen? What are the rules at home? How can I keep myself safe?
When am I most at risk?

4
Focus on outdoors
What is good about my outdoor world? Where do I play? Where do I go with my family and friends? What do I like about roads, cars, bikes, rivers? What do I need to practise? How do accidents happen? What is good about staying with what I know and where I am known?
When am I most at risk?

5
Focus on people
Who are my special people? How do I recognise them? What do my special people do to make me feel safe and happy? What do they do to make me upset, cross and worried? How do I make them happy, sad, cross and worried? What happens when I say 'No', 'Please don't', 'I'll ask'? Which people make me feel unsafe? How do I say 'No' to them? How do I find someone safe to help me? Who has the job of keeping me safe? What is my job?
When am I most at risk?

Key messages
for keeping myself safe

Learn:

• who you are, where you live and who is at home;

• where you are, who is with you and who is in charge of you;

• about some of the people whose job it is to help you keep safe and how you can help them;

• about the safe places to play and how to play safely;

• about the dangerous places and what makes them dangerous;

• who are the safe people to be with;

• to stay close to what you know and what you are happiest with;

• to ask for help;

• to say 'No', 'Stop', 'I'll ask';

• to tell people what happened and when and where it happened, and how to go on telling until someone listens.

Understand:

• that you and your body are special, valuable and unique;

• that you don't cause all the adult problems around you;

• that it is good to keep some secrets, but bad to keep others;

• the difference between real and pretend;

• that asking and telling someone are the best things to do if you are worried, scared or unsure;

• that getting told off is different from other dangers;

• that accidents are sometimes caused by what you do, sometimes caused by what others do and sometimes no one is to blame.

Practise:

• the skills you need to do things and to go to places safely;

• the rules about people, places and things;

• playing safely, having fun and feeling safe.

Share these key messages with parents, families and people in the community so that they can support and reinforce them.

Keeping myself safe

Key words

pretend real friend pleased worried safe secret tell magic imagination

Content box 1

1

Focus on feelings
What do I think I have to keep safe from? How do I think I keep safe? What is real and what is pretend? Which threats, promises and secrets are real and which are pretend? Do I always have to keep secrets? Which secrets are good and which are bad? Who can I ask for help? If I tell someone will I get into trouble?
When am I most at risk?

Activity 1 *What do I think I have to keep safe from?*

- Drawing and painting. Talking together. Making a display or wall story. Classroom play.

- Class and group activity.

Invite the children to draw or paint pictures of themselves keeping safe, and things they are keeping safe from. Explore their views of what the hazards are and how they think they could deal with them. Although some imaginary dangers will seem very real to some children, this could be a time to help them distinguish between real and pretend dangers. Bring their illustrations together to form a shared display or wall story. Write captions for them. You can use this chart to prompt the children to talk about the kinds of safety strategies they would use in different situations. Help the children to practise these strategies through classroom play.

Activity 2 *What is real and what is pretend?*

- Talking together. Sharing stories and television programmes.

- Class and group activity.

Many of the stories read to children at this age, and some television programmes viewed both in and out of school, can provide starting points for distinguishing between real and imaginary characters and situations.

Children can look for stories where solutions are reached by magic, where threats and promises can seem impossible, unbelievable or dreadful. In other stories they can look for real problems, threats and promises. Stories and programmes about real people who have imaginary friends, pets or toys which come alive when adults are not there make good starting points for exploring real and imaginary fears and secrets (an important theme in later stages).

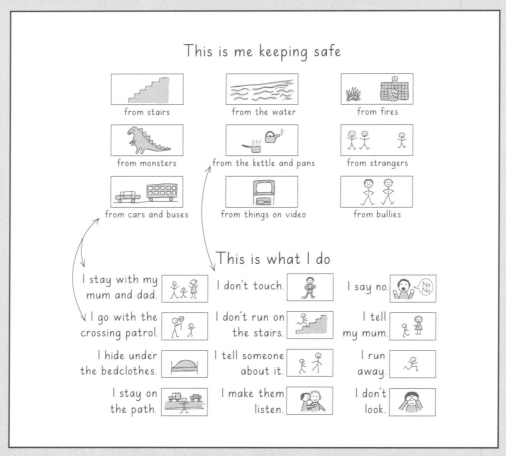

Real friends

This is my friend at school.

This is me playing with my dog. It's my friend.

This is my grown up friend in the shop.

These are my family friends.

Many of the children will have had experience of keeping safe secrets at home and school, and these can be shared to emphasise the fun and caring aspect of such secrets.

I had a safe secret and I didn't tell.

We hid my mum's present.
I didn't tell.

My teddy talks to me in bed.
I don't tell.

We're doing a concert for Christmas.
We aren't telling yet.

Benny cried at school.
I didn't tell anyone, only the teacher.

Our puppy wet the carpet.
We didn't tell.
He'd have got told off.

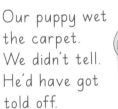

This is me keeping a safe secret.

The children could then begin to distinguish between different kinds of secrets. Talk together about:

– secrets kept from them (and how they felt about this);

– secrets accompanied by some kind of threat or promise.

! This will provide opportunities, where appropriate, for you to reinforce the difference between loving and non-loving secrets, and to emphasise the importance of telling someone and making someone listen when secrets are causing distress. **!**

Someone had a secret and didn't tell me.

My gran had a secret and she didn't tell me. It was a kitten. I was surprised.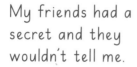

My mum had a secret and she didn't tell me. It was a new baby.

I liked it in the end. It was good.

My friends had a secret and they wouldn't tell me.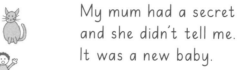

I cried. I didn't like it.

I had a secret and I did tell

The video at Billy's house scared me. They said not to tell, but I told my mum.

Some big boy bullies took my sweets. They said not to tell, but I told my teacher.

Someone tried to make me do things. They said they'd give me some sweets and not to tell – but I did tell.

This is me with a bad secret.

This is me feeling better when I told someone.

Keeping myself safe

Key words

know   practise   name   address   number   remember   describe   recognise

Content box 2

> **2**
>
> *Focus on me*
> *Who am I? Where am I?*
> *Where have I been? Who is*
> *(was) with me? Who is in*
> *charge of me? Where do I live?*
> *Who is there? How can I get*
> *there safely? What should I do*
> *when I am lost? What should I*
> *do to get help? What should I*
> *not do? How can I ask for*
> *help?*
> **When am I most at risk?**

Activity 1 *Who am I? Where do I live?*

- Classroom play. Drawing and painting. Making a display. Number recognition.

- Class and group activity.

Many different classroom activities can be used to help children practise saying who they are and where they live. In classroom play the theme of 'visitors' and 'visiting' can involve saying who you are, where you have come from and where you have been. Other examples include going to the doctor's surgery and ordering things by telephone.

You could give the children stand up name cards on which are written their names and addresses. These cards could be used by the children in a variety of ways, for example to label their work, to be incorporated into displays or to be part of play activities.

> Susie Smith
> 14 West Street
> Bigton

Invite the children to draw or paint pictures of their front doors. Display them, adding the number of the house in bold print. Play 'find your door' or 'find other people's doors'.

There are **cross-curricular links** with stories, poems and rhymes.

Ask the children what a character from a story would say if asked: 'Who are you? Where do you live?' For example, in *Jack and the Beanstalk*:

Jack: My name is Jack. I live in a cottage by a big tree.

Giant: I am the Giant. I live in a castle at the top of the tree.

Activity 2 *Where am I? Where am I going?*

- Drawing and painting. Talking together. Classroom play.
- Class or group activity.

Invite the children to draw or paint pictures of themselves in different places, at different times of the day, wearing different clothes and doing different things. Ask them to say where they are or where they are going and what they are doing. For example:

– I am at home in bed;

– I am going to the shops;

– I am at my Gran's house;

– I am at school, in the playground;

– I am going home.

Write the children's responses in speech bubbles and add them to their drawings.

Talk with the children about how important it is to know where they are and where they are going; to ask for help; and not to go off alone, or with another person. These themes can be explored further and practised through classroom play.

Activity 3 *What should I do when I am lost?*

■ Talking together. Stories and poems. Drawing.

■ Class or group activity, with opportunity for family work.

Invite the children to talk about the times when they, or someone they know, lost something. Tell them a story of your own too (children enjoy hearing of other people's experiences). Talk about how they felt, who helped them, if and where they found the lost item and how they felt about its return. There are many stories and poems which use this theme and these will provide good starting points.

Invite the children to talk about a time when they or someone they know was lost, or use a story or poem as a starting point for exploring the feeling of being lost.

Ask the children to describe or draw the place where they became lost. Encourage them to talk about what happened and who, if anyone, helped. Was it someone they knew or a stranger?

Explore with the children safe strategies for getting help, for example in the street, in a store, in a car park or at a bus station.

We got lost

Sam got lost in the supermarket. The shop lady lifted him up to find his mum.

Anna got lost in the market. She asked a kind looking lady with some children.

Ali got lost near his house. His big brother found him.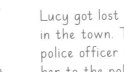

Lucy got lost in the town. The police officer took her to the police station until her dad came.

Tracy got lost at school. A midday helper found her.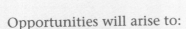

Opportunities will arise to:

– identify the 'safe' people in your community and talk about how we recognise them and ask for help;

– talk about safe people, how they help and the limits of that help;

– talk about possible dangers from unknown people or from known people who cause unease or fear;

– warn children about people who use phrases such as: 'I am lost' or 'I've lost my dog' as a ruse for enticing a child away, and the importance of saying 'No, I can't help', 'I'll go and ask someone'.

Provide opportunities for children to practise these skills and to share them with **families** and other people they know and trust.

Keeping myself safe

Key words

harm   hurt   dangerous   safe   rules   my job   responsibility

Content box 3

> **3**
>
> *Focus on indoors*
> *What is good about my home? Am I warm, fed and happy? Why must I be careful with fires, cookers, electricity, gas, television, stairs and medicines? How do accidents happen? What are the rules at home? How can I keep myself safe?*
> *When am I most at risk?*

Activity 1 — *What is good about my home?*

- Talking together. Writing, drawing, painting and role-play. Collecting and sorting pictures.

- Class and group activity, with opportunity for individual work and family work.

Before focusing on hazards in the home, it can be useful to look at items of household equipment, firstly in terms of what is good and useful about them, and secondly in terms of the possible dangers they present. Invite the children to think of the things and people in their homes which keep them warm, comfortable, happy and safe.

What is in my home?

windows to look out of	doors to go in and out	fires to warm you	people to look after you	chairs to sit on	cooker to cook on	bed to sleep in
knives and forks to eat your dinner	kettle to make tea	stairs to go up	lights	TV to watch	toys to play with	cupboards to put things in

---

Talk with the children about what makes these things and people good or useful. How would it be if there were no doors, windows, TV or people?

Ask the children to look again at these items and to say what could make each one unsafe. This could provide an opportunity for children to see the difference between things they might do which could cause accidents and things other people might do which could cause harm.

Look at strategies for keeping safe, for example *not* touching, switching, opening, playing about, jumping or running. Talk about putting things away; listening to what people say; saying if you are worried or scared and telling someone you trust, especially if people's actions or demands are causing distress.

Use talking, writing, painting and role-play to reinforce these safety strategies. Where appropriate, the children could begin to look at strategies they could use when they are alone, with friends, with family, with other adults or with strangers.

Invite the children to think and talk about the places in the home where accidents can happen, for example on the stairs, in the kitchen, in the bathroom and in the living room. Look at 'do's' and 'don'ts' in these places. Encourage the children to ask themselves: 'Is this a safe place to play?'

Ask the children to collect pictures from magazines of places to play and of children playing, and to sort them into these categories:

– safe places to play;

– unsafe places to play;

– children playing safely or in a safe place;

– children playing dangerously or in a dangerous place.

Invite the children to draw and paint their own pictures of safe places to play at home, at school and outdoors, and to say what they believe makes these places safe.

Invite the children to draw themselves playing safely in different places at home, at school and outdoors, alone or with friends, and to say what they think playing safely entails.

Provide opportunities for children to practise these skills and to share them with their **families** and friends.

Keeping myself safe

Content box 4

> **4**
>
> **Focus on outdoors**
> *What is good about my outdoor world? Where do I play? Where do I go with my family and friends? What do I like about roads, cars, bikes, rivers? What do I need to practise? How do accidents happen? What is good about staying with what I know and where I am known?*
> **When am I most at risk?**

Activity 1 — *What is good about my outdoor world?*

■ Talking together. Drawing and painting.

■ Class and group activity.

Explore with the children all the places they go – to play, to visit and to use – in the outdoor world. Talk about where they go; who takes them; who goes with them; what they do; what they like and don't like about going out; what makes it fun, interesting, exciting, boring, worrying and frightening.

Invite the children to talk about and illustrate the theme: 'We are going out. What can we see?' For example:

– in the playground we can see the climbing frame and the fence – what are the rules?

– in the garden we can see the gate, the shed and our toys – what are the rules?

– in the country we can see water, bridges and trees – what are the rules?

– in the street we can see cars, buses, people and shops – what are the rules?

– in the park we can see the lake, the trees and the swings – what are the rules?

Invite the children to think and talk about:

– the people they meet on their way to these places;

– the traffic and other hazards, for example roads, water, lack of pavements.

The children's responses and illustrations can be displayed as a focus for further activities on the theme of keeping safe.

Explore with the children the hazards or dangers they might encounter during their outdoor activities and what they see as the best ways of keeping themselves safe.

Invite the children to ask themselves these important questions:

! – is this a safe place to go?

    – should I go on my own?

    – should I go with someone I don't know?

    – is this a safe place to play?

If the answer is 'no' – don't go! **!**

Activity 2 *How do accidents happen?*

■ Talking together. Drawing and writing.

■ Class and group activity, with opportunity for individual work.

Ask the children to talk, draw and write about an everyday, minor accident, focusing on what caused it. Many young children believe that the cause of an accident lies in the object itself, rather than in the child's activity: 'cars run over you', 'bonfires burn you', 'rough ground makes you fall over'. It is important at this early stage to help the children see that some accidents are caused by what they do, and others are caused by what other people do. Make a note of the children's responses. Note the number of times the children blame themselves, blame someone else or put the blame on the object itself.

We have been looking at accidents

Ravi fell off the wall and hurt his knee. It was too high.

Martin ran across the road. He didn't look.

Emma's gran slipped on the ice. She didn't know it was slippery.

Some big boys pushed Benny off his bike. It wasn't an accident

Tamsin fell in the pool. It wasn't deep.

Jim tried to be superman. He couldn't fly.

Use the children's illustrations and writing as a starting point for asking:

– what made this accident?

– how did it happen?

– whose fault was it?

– what could the people have done to stop the accident happening?

This is a good time to remind children of the dangers of attempting to copy the actions of real or fantasy characters seen on television programmes.

Don't try copying things you see and saying I can jump off a bus like this.

Look with the children at what they see as ways of keeping safe in different places. Invite them to illustrate themselves keeping safe in places such as:

– the playground;

– the shops or shopping centre;

– on the way to and from school;

– near the road or river;

– in a car, on the bus, at the station;

– alone, with others, with strangers.

The children's perceptions of how they keep themselves safe will be very illuminating and will provide a starting point for activities which develop key skills for keeping safe, such as:

– knowing who they are, where they live, who is with them or looking after them and what that person is called;

– being able to name and describe (or illustrate) a street, a path, a pavement, a bridge, a crossing, traffic lights, a drive, an entry, a car park, a parked car;

– being able to distinguish different kinds of vehicles;

– being able to understand and explain (or illustrate) what they mean by 'alone', 'with someone', 'a grown up', 'on', 'off', 'by', 'near', 'far', 'close', 'across the road', 'to cross the road', 'stop', 'wait';

– recognising people who control the traffic and how they do this;

– practical skills – walking purposefully, stopping, waiting, looking, listening, recognising and naming sounds;

– practical skills – handling large toys, such as tricycles.

Ask the children to help you to build up a set of 'keeping myself safe' rules, emphasising these skills. Can they condense these rules into an 'everywhere' rule which will help to keep them safe wherever they are? This would be an opportunity to introduce the difference between rules (which are good advice) and laws (about traffic, car parking, etc.).

Keeping myself safe

Key words								
special	know	feelings	teach	touch	worry	my job	rules	help

Content box 5

5

Focus on people
Who are my special people?
How do I recognise them?
What do my special people do
to make me feel safe and
happy? What do they do to
make me upset, cross and
worried? How do I make them
happy, sad, cross and
worried? What happens when
I say 'No', 'Please don't', 'I'll
ask'? Which people make me
feel unsafe? How do I say 'No'
to them? How do I find
someone safe to help me?
Who has the job of keeping
me safe? What is **my** *job?*
When am I most at risk?

Activity 1 | *Who are my special people?*

- Talking. Drawing and painting. Classroom play. Writing. Making books.

- Class, group and individual activity.

Invite the children to talk about, describe, illustrate and dress up as some of the people who are special to them. Most children will have people at home or at school who they trust or admire and with whom they feel safe and have a special relationship. Exploring positive feelings of trust and safety and what these involve (and don't involve) can be a good way of enabling young children to distinguish between safe and unsafe people.

Ask the children to talk, illustrate and write (with your help) about:

- what their special people look like and how they pick them out in a crowd;

- what their special people do and say, or don't do and don't say.

The work resulting from these activities can be brought together to make individual, group or class books.

This basic work on what special people do and say can provide a framework for children to talk about the different ways in which people show they love and care about others. Children who sometimes dislike being hugged, kissed or touched by some people, or who are afraid or abused can, through these activities, be helped to talk about their feelings and concerns. The question of when it is important or appropriate to say 'No' in various forms such as: 'Please don't', 'I don't like that', 'I'd rather not' or 'I don't want to', is best approached in small group or one-to-one supportive situations. Parents and families will need to be aware of the reasons why children are exploring this topic.

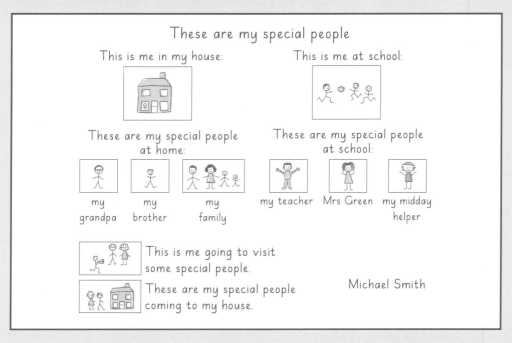

The children could illustrate themselves saying 'Yes, please' and 'No, thank you' to people at home, at school and in the neighbourhood. Ask them to explain what it is they are accepting, refusing or being asked to do. Opportunities may arise, or can be structured, to enable children to draw and talk about the more worrying aspects of saying 'Yes' and 'No', and to disclose pressures, fears, threats and abuse.

! This work can provide a starting point for introducing other material relating to child abuse and personal safety. Its major purpose, however, is to provide as many non-threatening, warm, sharing opportunities as possible, to encourage children to talk about things which bother them. It provides the first of a series of activities which enable the children to recognise risk and build up their own safety skills. **!**

Explore with the children ways in which they can make the job of keeping themselves safe easier for their special people. Talk with the children about the things they do, or might do, which would worry their special people. This could be an early introduction to being a good citizen.

When do my special people worry about me?

I ran off the pavement.
My mum was scared stiff.

I left my toys on the stairs
and my grandpa fell.
I cried.

I broke a window
and cut my hand.

I went off and
got lost.
They were cross.

I went home from
school on my own.
My teacher was
worried.

Ask the children about the things which their special people do which worry them and make them feel unsafe. Responses might include:

- leave us with babysitters;
- send us to bed;
- tell us off;
- tease us;

- scare us;
- cross the road at the wrong place;
- leave us alone in the car.

You can provide individual children with opportunities to reveal their own concerns during small group activities, when you can encourage a non-threatening sharing atmosphere.

Activity 2 *Who else has the job of keeping me safe?*

■ Talking together. Making a display of pictures and books. Visits and visitors.

■ Class and group activity.

Beyond the children's special people are a wider group of people who share the responsibility for keeping the children safe, but at this stage the children's perceptions may not extend far beyond the family, the crossing patrol and the police officer.

Explore with the children who it is they think keeps them safe wherever they are, indoors or outdoors. Make a note of the children's responses, prompting them with questions such as: 'But what if you get lost? ...if there is an accident? ... a fire? ... if you are at school?' Remind the children that they are the one person who is always there.

Help the children to make a display of pictures and books which shows the range of people in the community who, as good citizens, can and do help them. Invite the children to categorise these people using the question: 'How do I recognise them?' Look at the people who always wear a uniform, the people who sometimes do and the people who never do. How could these good citizens help the children keep safe?

This would be a good time to plan safety-related visits and visitors to increase the children's awareness of the roles of those people who keep them safe.

Follow-up activities which focus on questions such as: 'What do I do to help? ... to make them pleased? ... worried? ... angry?' are particularly important in enabling children to begin to be aware of their own responsibilities.

We are learning to be good citizens

This is our crossing patrol.

She came to talk to us today.

This is me making the crossing patrol pleased.

This is me making the crossing patrol worried.

I am waiting until she says NOW

I am crossing in the wrong place.

We are going to play crossing patrol.
We have got a coat and a lollipop stick.
We are helping people who help us.

There are **cross-curricular links** with:

– topic work in citizenship;

– the wider theme of people who help;

– stories, poems and rhymes;

– classroom play.

Reflection and action

Look back with the children at all they have learned about being and staying safe, and about keeping their feelings from being hurt and telling people how they feel.

- Remind them of the many people they have discovered who have the job of keeping them safe day and night.
- Ask them what they can do, as good citizens, to make these people's jobs easier.
- Remind them that they are getting better at this and ask them to give some examples of their growing skills.
- Pick out some 'keeping safe' activities relevant to the children, your school and the community, and ask the children to practise them and set a good example to other people.

Key theme 3: Me and my relationships

The five content boxes on page 81 each have a distinctive focus and act as starting points for the classroom activities. The questions in each content box stimulate discussion and help you to build on previous skills and knowledge and to identify where the children are in their understanding.

It is important that you select and extend the classroom activities according to: your PSHE or PSD and Citizenship programmes; your school's mission statement regarding the values central to your school; your school's behaviour policy; your programme for Assembly and/or corporate acts of Worship; your Healthy School initiatives; your school's sex education policy and programme.

Focus of teaching
- Recognising the importance of their different networks of people in which they live and work, and their roles in these networks.
- Understanding the importance of friendship.
- Recognising the dangers which can result from pressure from friends.
- Expressing love, care and feeling special in human relationships.
- Exploring loss, separation, grief and the importance of memories.
- Recognising that they have relationships with their environments and a growing role and responsibility for a happy, safe environment for all.
- Recognising that feelings can affect actions.

Key skills and competencies
Describing people, places, situations; naming of relations and relationships, friends and friendships; recognising inter-relationships; valuing others' feelings, preferences, property; understanding and naming stages in lifecycle; empathy; retelling in sequence.

Citizenship opportunities
The theme of learning to value people's property and feelings is central to citizenship. There will be opportunities for visits to and from people who are involved in protecting and improving the physical environment. Many of the key teaching points can be put into the playground and classroom ground-rules and behaviour policies and practised there.

Links with children's literature
Stories where characters are born, grow up, go out into the world. Stories about new babies and their impact on the family. Stories where characters have different family lifestyles and activities. Stories about the very young and the very old learning from each other.

Me and my relationships

1

Focus on special people
What are the things I treasure most? When and how do I use them? How do I take care of them? How do I feel if I lose them or they get spoilt? How am I like other people? How am I different? How am I special? Who are my special people? What do my special people do to make me happy or angry? What do I do to make them happy or angry?

2

Focus on friends and friendship
Who are my friends? What do I like best about my friends? What do my friends like about me? Can grown-ups be my friends? Do I have to keep promises and secrets if my friends say so? How do I say 'No' to them? Are pretend friends OK – can a pet be a friend? How do I look after my friends?

3

Focus on feelings
How can I tell how people are feeling? How can people tell how I am feeling? What kinds of things make me feel happy, sad or worried? Who and what makes us feel better? How do I feel when I lose something? How do I feel when my special people go away or die? Why don't people ask me how I feel? Who and what helps me when I feel like this?

4

Focus on memories
What makes things such as seeds, plants, animals and babies grow? What do they need to help them grow? What do I remember about being born and growing? What helped me to grow? What do other people remember about me? Do I remember the first time I did something? Who helped me? What is the happiest thing I remember? Who was there? Why was it so happy? Can my family and friends help me to remember things?

5

Focus on special places
Where are my special places in the classroom, at home and outside? What makes them special? What do I do there? Am I on my own, or with people? Is it safe to be there? Who knows I'm there? Is it a happy place? What keeps places special and happy? How can I help to keep my special places happy, healthy, clean and safe?

Key messages

for me and my relationships

Learn:

- how to find and tell a safe person if people hurt you, bully you, or if you are worried;

- how to say 'No' if people touch you and you don't like it or it worries you;

- to respect other people's families, friends, feelings and special places;

- to talk to your special people about how you feel;

- to take care of your feelings.

Understand:

- that just as your special people make you happy, sad or worried, you do the same to them;

- that most special people love and care for you all the time and will always help you;

- that when special people go away or die it may be very sad but it is not your fault;

- that people are born, grow up and then can have their own families;

- that pets and people die, and this makes us sad;

- that there is only one of you and that makes you very special.

Practise:

- talking about your feelings and other people's;

- taking care of the people, places and things you care about.

Share these key messages with parents, families and people in the community so that they can support and reinforce them.

Me and my relationships

Key words

special   same   different   treasures   feelings   share   tell   networks

Content box 1

1

Focus on special people
What are the things I treasure most? When and how do I use them? How do I take care of them? How do I feel if I lose them or they get spoilt? How am I like other people? How am I different? How am I special? Who are my special people? What do my special people do to make me happy or angry? What do I do to make them happy or angry?

Activity 1 *What are the things I treasure most?*

■ Making and displaying a collection. Talking together. Drawing and writing.

■ Class or group and individual activity.

Ask the children to help to make and display a collection of special things, both personal and classroom treasures, for example a new toy, an old and much loved toy, a photograph, some shells, a stick, a tin, a special piece of clothing, a book, a 'jewel'.

Invite the children to name and talk about these treasures as they are collected. Ask them to try to put into words what it is that makes seemingly ordinary things special to someone: point out the ones which are shiny and new and easily recognised as 'treasures', and the ones which are old, worn out and broken, but are still valued.

The items could be labelled, for example: 'This is special to Alice', and grouped, for example: 'These are old', 'These are new'. Talk with the children about their treasures. Where do they come from? When do the children need or want them? Do they share them, hide them or keep them for their own use?

Ask the children to talk, draw and write (using you as their 'scribe' as necessary) about the way they take care of their treasures. How do they keep them safe? How do they feel if they lose them or they are thrown away? How can they explain to other people that these things are so special?

Katie

This is me when I found my old teddy

Activity 2 *How am I special?*

- Talking together. Drawing and painting. Making a collage.
- Class or group and individual activity, with opportunity for family work.

Talk with the children about their classroom. How is it different in appearance from other classrooms? How is it different because of the people in it? What happens in their classroom? Look with the children at the people in the class who make us smile, laugh, bring things to show us, tell good stories and jokes, sing, help, paint exciting pictures and look after the plants and animals.

Invite the children to contribute paintings, drawings and photographs of themselves, and to help you make a collage on the theme of 'our class'.

Ask the children to think about what is special about each person in the class, for example their names, what they are good at, what they like doing.

Talk with the children about the things they can do for themselves, and about the things they are getting better at. These can either be practical or emotional achievements, for example not getting upset.

Family work: this activity could be extended through family work to include the things children are learning to do, or need help with out of school.

Activity 3 *Who are my special people?*

■ Talking together. Drawing and writing. Making books or charts.

■ Class or group and individual activity, with opportunity for family work.

This is a way of introducing the children to the idea of themselves at the centre of a network of special people (who also have their own networks).

Talk with the children about all the people who are special to them. Ask them to draw and label them. Invite them to tell their group or class about their special people at home, at school or elsewhere. What do they do together? What do they share? What do they say to them? How often do they see them? What do they look like? How do they speak?

Help the children to make their own books or charts about themselves and their network. These could be displayed or shared so that the children can see that, while they are often similar to each other, each of them is unique.

There are **cross-curricular links** with language work.

Extend the children's vocabulary of relations and relationships by providing them with opportunities to talk about their extended families, including the people they have left behind and the people who are new.

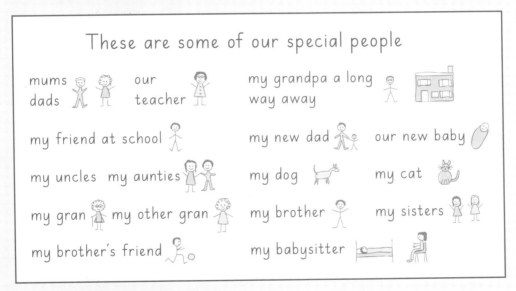

Ask the children: 'What do your special people do to make you happy?' Their answers may focus on material things, such as giving presents and sweets, or be more concerned with playing together, loving, caring, not teasing or not getting cross. Next, you could explore what the children think their special people do to make them upset, sad or angry. This is an opportunity to widen the vocabulary the children use to describe their feelings, and to deepen their understanding of the impact of other people's behaviour on themselves. Opportunities may arise for children to reveal experiences which frightened or threatened them or made them uneasy.

Invite the children to talk about their special people, or person, and what they do to make their special people happy. Record the children's ideas in a way that enables their views to be easily shared among the children and their families.

We are making our special people happy

We are helping them wash up.

We are making them laugh.

We are keeping healthy and happy.

We are giving them a cuddle.

We are playing together.

We are sending them a letter.

We are telling them how we feel.

This could be an opportunity to explain that pressure from people, special or otherwise, to make them happy in ways which cause the children distress must be resisted and reported.

Explore what the children think they do to make their special people sad, upset or angry. Emphasise that these are emotions all of us experience.

There are opportunities to reinforce or introduce 'keeping safe' messages, such as:

– adults can and do get upset and angry when children put themselves in danger;

– there are times when children have to say 'No' to adults, even though this may appear to make that adult sad or angry. Remind them of their work in keeping themselves safe.

Family work: families may find their children's views on relationships very revealing. It is important, wherever possible, that this work is taken home to be shared and extended there.

Me and my relationships

Content box 2

> **2**
>
> *Focus on friends and friendship*
> *Who are my friends? What do I like best about my friends? What do my friends like about me? Can grown-ups be my friends? Do I have to keep promises and secrets if my friends say so? How do I say 'No' to them? Are pretend friends OK – can a pet be a friend? How do I look after my friends?*

Activity 1 *Who are my friends?*

- Talking together. Drawing. Making a chart.

- Class or group and individual activity, with opportunity for family work.

The opportunity to choose one's own friends is an important step in the first years of school. Some children may previously have been told or expected to make friends without being given any choice. Others may have been told that the arrival of a new baby or new brothers and sisters will mean having new friends, and this may not have been so. It can be helpful to explore the children's own views of what a friend is and does, and what friendship means.

Imaginary or fictional friends may have been, or may still be, part of the children's fantasy life, and this can be a starting point for exploring aspects of friendship.

Our friends

listen to each other

sit together

play together

WE

like each other

share things

help each other

go home together

There are **cross-curricular links** with literature. Many picture storybooks, stories and poems for young children have friendship as a theme, featuring both real and imaginary friends. Children will enjoy thinking about the stories to discover why a character needed or wanted a friend, whether or not that friend was found, whether or not it was a real or imaginary friend, the difference which the friendship made, etc.

Family work: invite the children to ask their families whether they had imaginary friends when they were young.

Invite the children to draw the friends they have at school and to talk about them. Who are they? What do they do together? What do they share with them? Help them to make a 'friendship chart'. The children could contribute their own illustrations, or pictures from magazines, to the chart.

Ask the children what they like best about their friends. (Answers are likely to include aspects of appearance and personality.) A more difficult but important question to ask them is: 'What do your friends like about you?' In answering this question, the children will have opportunities to reinforce positive images of themselves as people who are valued. For example: 'I always play with her', 'I wait for him', 'I'm good at helping him', 'I lend him my things', 'I make him laugh', 'She likes me', 'She is always my friend'.

Activity 2 *Can grown-ups be my friends?*

- Talking together.

- Class or group activity.

Explore with the children the idea of having grown-ups as friends. Is this a different kind of friendship? Include people inside and outside their network of special people, and people they meet on a more informal basis. Talk about what makes being friends with these people so special. What do they do with the children? (For example, do they take them out on special occasions?) Where do they go? What makes them special friends? Could they go to them if they were lost or upset?

Our grown-up friends

The crossing patrol.
She knows our names.
She talks to us when she sees
us in the supermarket.
She keeps her things at school.

My big brother Alexander
He takes me to see football
and he buys me a hot dog.

My aunty Rose next door
She babysits me and we
stay up late. I keep it a
secret but she tells my dad.

My uncle Phil
He takes me fishing.
He lets me do it.
I'm good at it.

Mrs Kalinsky
She takes us to church in
the minibus every week
and sings all the time.

This would be a good time to introduce the idea of trusting special people. For example, special people they can trust are people who are kind, fun, don't frighten or threaten them and who stop teasing or tickling when asked.

The children could go on to explore what these special grown-up friends help them to do, for example learn and see new things. What do the grown-ups ask them to do? What if a grown-up asked them to keep a secret? Would this make the children feel grown up? This would be a good time to look again at keeping secrets and promises. (See Keeping Myself Safe, pages 65 and 66.)

Some children may want to talk about times when people turned out to be not such good friends – they may have broken their promises, threatened, bullied or abused them in some way. Encourage the children to share this and their feelings. Talk with the children about fairness and honesty.

Not such good friends

Bruno said I could have a go if I gave him my sweets, but he ran off. That wasn't fair. He wasn't honest.

My big sister wanted me to tell a fib. I was scared. I didn't know what to do. That wasn't fair.

My uncle Len wouldn't stop tickling me and I cried. He should have stopped when I asked.

Ellie didn't like it when I said no. She doesn't come round any more. She wouldn't play fair.

Activity 3 *Can a pet be a friend?*

- Talking together. Drawing, painting or collecting pictures.
- Class or group and individual activity.

Invite the children to talk about domestic and classroom pets. Who looks after them? When? How? Ask the children whether they know of people in the neighbourhood who have pets, in particular people who live alone and have a pet as a companion.

Remind the children of all the things they said that they could do and enjoy with their friends. Can pets do the same things, or more?

You can:

- play with them;
- talk to them;
- hug them;
- share sweets;
- go out with them;
- stay in with them;
- look after them;
- teach them things.

Pets can:

- make you laugh;
- listen to you;
- love you;
- look after you;
- keep you company;
- play with you;
- make you cross.

Ask them to illustrate this with their own drawings or paintings or by collecting pictures from magazines.

Ask the children to think about times when pets seem to be not such good friends, for example when they scratch, bite, go off with someone else or steal. Contrast this with the fun and pleasure they give us.

Draw the activity to a conclusion by looking at the everyday responsibility of keeping pets happy and healthy, regardless of how busy or tired the pet's owners might be.

Me and my relationships

feelings   tell   share   explain   listen   remember   left out   questions

Content box 3

> **3**
>
> *Focus on feelings*
> *How can I tell how people are feeling? How can people tell how I am feeling? What kinds of things make me feel happy, sad or worried? Who and what makes us feel better? How do I feel when I lose something? How do I feel when my special people go away or die? Why don't people ask me how I feel? Who and what helps me when I feel like this?*

Activity 1 *How can I tell how people are feeling?*

■ Talking together. Collecting and sorting pictures. Drawing and painting. Mime and movement. Making a wall story or collage.

■ Class or group and individual activity.

A useful resource for exploring and deepening children's understanding of feelings and emotions is a collection of pictures of people laughing, crying, looking sad, worried, angry, lonely, frightened, etc. This collection can be a starting point for small group activities in which children are encouraged to talk about some of the pictures, thus increasing their vocabulary for describing emotions.

Invite the children to sort the pictures into groups, using their own criteria. With your help the children can make labels for each group, for example: 'These are laughing faces'. They can then add more pictures to the collection, for example photographs and pages from magazines, and their own drawings and paintings.

Explore in mime and movement the facial expressions and body language of laughter, sadness, unhappiness, anger, fright, etc.

Invite the children to paint pictures of themselves or other people showing some of these feelings and to display these as a wall story or collage.

Talk with the children about times when they have felt like this, and why. When they felt unhappy, what made them feel better?

Activity 2   *How do I feel when I lose something?*

■ Talking together. Classroom play. Making a 'circle of feelings'.

■ Class or group activity.

Suggest themes for the playhouse or play area on losing something, for example a pet, a toy, a parcel or something special and important. Encourage the children to reflect on some of their feelings when they discovered a loss. What do they say? How is the problem solved?

Make a 'circle of feelings', using speech bubbles, based on this activity. Invite the children to illustrate it using pictures from the collection they made in Activity 1, or their own drawings and paintings.

Encourage the children to talk about how they feel when their special people leave them or go away for some reason (permanently or temporarily), or die. This is particularly important since many young children experiencing such a loss may be excluded or protected from expressions of grief, or given compensatory presents to distract them. This can result in them feeling that they have been left out of something important, and may leave them with many unanswered questions, such as: 'Was it my fault?'

Talk with the children about what makes them feel better. Responses might include:

– my dad told me what had happened – we had a cry together;

– my granny gave me a big hug;

– my best friend said I could stay over at her house;

– I told my teacher about it and she was sad too;

– my Uncle Fred said I would feel better soon;

– my Mum said it wasn't my fault.

It is important that children learn about loss and grief, if possible before it happens to them or their friends, so that they can cope with their own feelings and be sensitive to the feelings of others. To do this they need to experience and share some of these feelings in the safe context of the classroom, through talking together, role-play and stories.

Me and my relationships

Key words

born   families   networks   parents   babies   love   care   remember

Content box 4

4

Focus on memories
What makes things such as seeds, plants, animals and babies grow? What do they need to help them grow? What do I remember about being born and growing? What helped me to grow? What do other people remember about me? Do I remember the first time I did something? Who helped me? What is the happiest thing I remember? Who was there? Why was it so happy? Can my family and friends help me to remember things?

Activity 1 *What makes things grow? What makes me grow?*

■ Talking together. Drawing. Collecting pictures.

■ Class or group and individual activity.

Cross-curricular link: this part of the work links with early science activities in which children can be encouraged to observe and categorise living things as they change and grow.

Look at growing things in and around the school and classroom: seeds, plants, animals and the children themselves. Are any of the children expecting the birth of a baby brother or sister? This might be a good time to talk about how new babies are born and cared for.

What do things need to grow?

Seeds and plants need:

  water

  soil

  sun

  air

Seeds don't need:

  mums

  clothes

  houses

Puppies, kittens
and baby hamsters
need:

  love and care

  mums for milk

  mums for looking after

  sleep

  air

Puppies don't need:

  clothes

Babies need:

  love and care

  a family

  air   sun

  sleep love

  someone to look after them

  milk and food

Babies don't need:

  soil

Make a note of the children's ideas of what makes these things grow. Sort them into groups and help the children to illustrate them.

Invite the children to make a collection of pictures of babies and young children. They could include photographs of themselves, or their own drawings of themselves, when they were small. Display these as a starting point for talking about their memories of the people involved in helping them to grow up. What did people do to help them? For example loving, caring, protecting, teaching and providing.

Activity 2 *What do I remember about being born and growing?*

- Talking together. Making a class book.

- Class or group and individual activity, with opportunity for family work.

Ask the children whether they can remember being born or *before* they were born. (Some children will be certain they can and these memories, if shared, can be very illuminating.)

Do the children remember:

– being in cots, prams or pushchairs?

– learning to walk, talk, feed themselves, dress and undress?

– going on trains and buses?

– going to playgroup, the child minder or the nursery?

– going to hospital?

Who was with them?

Family work: where appropriate, invite members of the children's families to contribute their memories of the child growing up. Memory, and other people's memories, form an important part of a person's sense of identity.

Exploring this aspect of growing up can help each child to become aware of the network of relationships in which he or she is involved and the place he or she holds in that network.

The children could make a class book, or set of books, of these memories.

Family work: ask the children and their families to remember some of their happiest moments. Encourage the children to share these memories.

Cross-curricular links: in trying to pin down what happened, who was there, what made them happy, etc., the children will be tackling a wide range of language and historical skills including description, organising their thoughts, chronology and listening. Repeat this activity again with family help, asking the children to explore other memories, for example the funniest, the most exciting and the saddest things they can remember. If the children are helped to explore the past in a non-threatening way and encouraged to explain why they remember specific occasions so well, they and their families (and yourself) may all gain some valuable insights.

Me and my relationships

Key words

special different like safe happy neighbourhood environment rules responsibility

Content box 5

> **5**
>
> **Focus on special places**
> *Where are my special places in the classroom, at home and outside? What makes them special? What do I do there? Am I on my own, or with people? Is it safe to be there? Who knows I'm there? Is it a happy place? What keeps places special and happy? How can I help to keep my special places happy, healthy, clean and safe?*

Activity 1 *Where are my special places?*

- Talking together. Drawing and writing. Links with literature.

- Class or group and individual activity, with opportunity for family work.

Cross-curricular links: this part of the work links with environmental studies and children's literature. A useful starting point would be a story or poem about animals who have their own special places in which to live or hide. Ask the children about the special places where their pets sleep. Ask them where their own special places are and why. Start with areas in the classroom, for example in the playhouse, in the book corner.

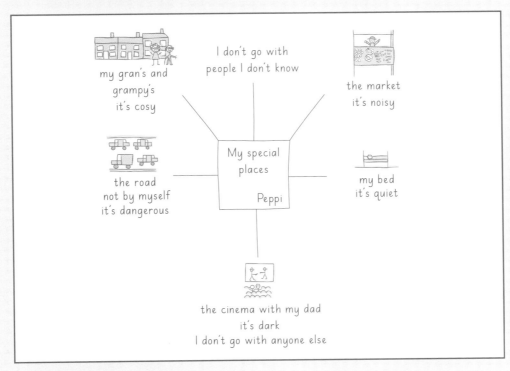

Ask the children where their other special places are, for example at home, in the playground and in the neighbourhood. Talk with the children about what makes these places special and safe. Who takes them there and what do they do? Which people would they not go with? What are the rules of the place? How do the rules make us feel happier? Ask the children to put this information onto individual charts. Write for them as necessary.

Family work: encourage the children to take their charts home, and ask their families to add to them with drawing or writing.

Explore with the children what they do in their special places. What do they enjoy most? What makes the place a happy one? In what ways can they, or other people, make their special places happy, clean, tidy and safe? What do they do if there is a problem? Who do they tell? What do they say?

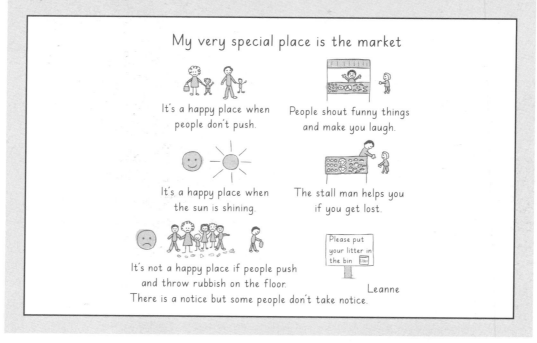

Reflection and action

Look back with the children at all they have learned.
- Remind them that everyone is unique and special and that this uniqueness is something to value.
- Remind them that they are growing up and growing more responsible, and that their networks of people will be getting bigger.
- Remind them that friends are important but sometimes friends can try to persuade them to do things which are possibly dangerous.

Look back at what babies need so that they can grow up happily and safely. Remind the children that love and care between people is something very important and that some day they may be parents themselves and want to teach their children to be loving.
- Remind them that they also have to value and care for the places around them so that these are safe, happy places, and so that the children using them can be safe and happy there.
- Ask them to practise being loving, caring and safe.

Ages 6 and 7

Healthy Lifestyles

Key themes

Key themes: Overview

The overview below offers planned routes for classroom activities that develop key Personal, Social and Health Education and Citizenship skills, drawing on the Action Planners on pages 100, 101 and 102. The Action Planners comprise a series of structured questions that form a spiral curriculum of teaching and learning goals for the 6–7 age range

Key themes	Content boxes
1 Healthy lifestyles • Healthy places, exercise, rest and personal hygiene • Personal responsibilities	9 → 7 → 26 (see page 103)
2 Healthy eating • Making informed choices	3 → 34 → 23 (see page 113)
3 Feelings and relationships • Self-esteem and family life	14 → 20 → 36 (see page 121)

Citizenship and **Emotional Wellbeing** are covered by these key themes. The content boxes act as starting points for the classroom activities set out in this section. You will find that the questions in each content box stimulate discussion and help you to identify where the children are in their understanding.

It is important that you select and extend the classroom activities according to:

• your PSHE or PSD and Citizenship programmes;
• your Healthy School initiatives.

The additional themes listed below provide further suggestions to develop and extend key health skills. They plot an alternative route through the Action Planner key content.

Additional themes	Content boxes
1 Keeping safe • Growing responsibility for self	12 → 27 → 29
2 How my body works and changes • Early understanding of body systems	4 → 8 → 11 → 5
3 The world of medicines and drugs • Increased awareness of the real world	2 → 13 → 29 → 35

Me and looking after myself

1

My special body, my special face, my size, shape and colour. Are we the same? Are we different?

2

It's what I do to my body that makes and keeps it healthy. What do I do? What do I put onto it and into it? Who tells me to do this?

3

What do I eat? What do I like to eat and drink? Why do I eat? What meals do people eat? When? Where? Who tells me what to eat and drink? When can I choose for myself? What helps me to choose? What helps me to stick to my choice or to change my mind? For example TV, friends, learning about food.

4

How do I think my body is changing? How has it changed since I was a baby and since I came to school? What makes it change and grow?

5

Am I feeling good about my body? Am I enjoying what it can do? What can I make it do? How does this make me feel?

What are the words I need to know:

■ to describe formally parts of the body? (What are *my* words?)

■ to describe how these parts work?

■ to understand my own responsibilities?

6

What do I do to look after myself each day? For example personal hygiene, keeping safe, exercise, sleep, rest, play, work.

7

What do I think I do to make and keep myself healthy? What else do I need to know about being healthy? What is a healthy day for me?

8

What do I think is inside me? What is my skeleton like – and my heart? Where are the different systems in my body? How do I think they work?

9

How do I think healthy people look? feel? live? What is their message to us? What about not so healthy people? What is my message to them? What do healthy people do some of the time? all the time? never? What is a healthy day for them?

10

What do not so healthy people do some of the time? all the time? never? How do they look? feel? live? What is my message to them?

11

What happens to my body when I exercise? What can I see happening? What do I think happens inside me when I exercise?

12

What do I think I have to keep safe from at home? at school? outside? How do I think I keep safe?

13

What happens when I sleep and rest? What happens when I am ill? What happens when I am given medicines and injections? What can I do – or not do – to get better?

Me, my family and my friends

14

What makes me the same as you? What are the feelings we all share? For example being happy, sad, cheerful, afraid, uneasy, shy, clumsy. What makes us different? How does it feel to be different?

15

What do we all (children and grown-ups) do? For example love, quarrel, lose friends, pets, treasures; grow, grow up, grow older; work, play, get tired.

16

How does it feel to be like other people? How does it feel to be different?

17

How do you know I am me? How do you know how I feel? What tells you? my face? my body language? my voice? What can you do to understand how I feel? For example listen, look, hug and help.

18

Who are my special people? Who are your special people? What do they do for me? say to me? tell me? How do I show them they are special? How do they show me I am special?

What are the words I need to know:

- to describe my network of relationships?
- to tell people how I feel?
- to describe how other people feel?
- to describe loss and grief?
- to tell people I feel confident?
- to describe being special and valued?
- to describe how other people are special?

19

What do I do to make my special people happy? happier? worried? angry? better? What do they do to make me feel happy? worried? angry? better?

20

What makes me feel good about myself and my days? How do I feel when I feel good? What can I do to help make myself feel good?

21

What can I do when I am frightened? lost? bullied? upset? What can I learn to do? How can I say 'No', 'Yes', 'I can't', 'I won't', 'I don't' and 'Stop'?

22

How does it feel when special people or things change, leave, are lost or die? Who can help me to understand? What can they do?

23

What makes some of my days special? For example good experiences, happenings, surprises, food. What are the days I remember and the days I look forward to? For example happy times, sad times, landmarks.

24

What makes other people's days better or special? Getting on with other people: how can I make their days special? For example listening, visiting, caring.

25

How does it feel when I've done something new or difficult? helped someone? mastered a problem? enjoyed something?

Me, my community and my environment

26

What do I think makes places healthy or not so healthy?

27

How do I think I keep myself safe? Whose job is it to keep me safe? What's my part of this job?

28

Where do I live? Where do you live? Who else lives here? there? nearby? How are we all the same? How are we different? What do other people do? Where do they all meet? For example on the street, in shops, in pubs, in clubs, in church. Where do I meet them?

29

Who looks after me and my health and safety? Where do they work? Can we go and see? Whose job is it to keep me healthy and safe? Is it my job too? How do I recognise (and trust) these people? For example, I go by what they wear and say and by what they tell me to do. Do I feel good, or not so good, about what they do?

30

Who keeps safe the places that I go to? What is their message to us? How can I help?

What are the words I need to know:

■ to name people and their jobs?

■ to describe being sure and not so sure?

■ to describe people's responsibilities?

■ to recognise the rules and laws?

■ to describe my network of people?

■ to talk about danger and dangerous objects?

■ to ask for help and instruction?

31

How do I know I am growing up? Where can I go now on my own? with friends? with grown-ups? Can I decide for myself? Who and when must I ask?

32

Special occasions at school, at home and in the neighbourhood, for me and for others: meetings, parades, fetes, carnivals, celebrations. What makes them special for me? for you? for others?

33

What can I do to help the people who have few or no special times?

34

Who keeps food clean and safe? What can I do to help?

35

What makes some places special? For example quiet places, noisy and crowded places, places for being alone, places for sharing, secret places, real and imaginary places. What are safe places for dangerous things? For example medicine cabinets, cupboards, handbags, shops, sheds. What dangerous things can I see, reach and touch?

36

Who are our special people and friends? What do they do and say? What do we do together? What do we share or keep secret? What do I like about them and like doing with them? What makes me scared sometimes or uneasy? Who can I tell?

37

What do I think makes things, places and people safe or not so safe?

Key theme 1: Healthy lifestyles

9

How do I think healthy people look? feel? live? What is their message to us? What about not so healthy people? What is my message to them? What do healthy people do some of the time? all the time? never? What is a healthy day for them?

7

What do I think I do to make and keep myself healthy? What else do I need to know about being healthy? What is a healthy day for me?

26

What do I think makes places healthy or not so healthy?

These content boxes are from the Action Planners on pages 100, 101 and 102.

Focus of teaching
- Recognising and valuing differences in their own and others' lifestyles and cultures relating to health.
- Heightened awareness and knowledge of the components of a healthy lifestyle and their increasing responsibilities.
- Developing and using a framework for evaluating healthy lifestyles.
- Recognising the need for up-to-date factual information on which to base choices and decisions.
- Recognising that we all have a right of access to a safe, healthy environment, but with this come responsibilities and the necessity to stop and think.

Key skills and competencies
Listening, speaking, discussion; extending vocabulary of past and present; categorising according to criteria; comparing and evaluating; setting up a survey and drawing out information; decision making.

Citizenship opportunities
Opportunities to participate in school and community health initiatives and environmental projects.

Links with children's literature
Stories where characters set out to find or create a better environment or defend their playgrounds against others.

Healthy lifestyles

Content box 9

9

How do I think healthy people look? feel? live? What is their message to us? What about not so healthy people? What is my message to them? What do healthy people do some of the time? all the time? never? What is a healthy day for them?

Activity 1 *How do healthy people look?*

- ■ Talking together. Drawing. Making a display.
- ■ Shared or individual activity.

Invite the children to show, with facial expressions, body posture and movements, how healthy people feel, look and move. Contrast this with how not so healthy people feel, look and move. Invite the children to draw pictures of healthy and not so healthy people and to explain to others how these people look and how healthy and not so healthy characteristics are portrayed.

Ask the children to help make decisions about displaying the pictures. Should all the pictures of healthy people be grouped together, or should pictures be displayed in pairs showing one healthy and one not so healthy person?

Activity 2 *What is their message?*

- ■ Talking together. Drawing and writing.
- ■ Small group and individual activity.

Provide some large cut-out speech and thought bubbles. Look again at the display of pictures from Activity 1. Invite the children to empathise with the characters they have

drawn and described. Can they make themselves look like these characters and try to feel as they might feel?

What might the characters be saying? Involve the children in deciding on the messages to write in the speech and thought bubbles.

Read and reread the messages together, experimenting with different kinds of voices.

What kind of message do the children have for the not so healthy characters? Make a note of some of their ideas. Invite each child to draw herself or himself and write (or dictate) a message for the not so healthy characters. It is important to use 'not so healthy' rather than 'unhealthy' to avoid polarisation.

This is my message:

Do lots of exercise.

Alexis

This is my message:

Go to bed early.

Becky

This is my message:

Clean your teeth all the days.

Carl

Activity 3 *What do healthy people do?*

■ Talking together. Sorting. Drawing. Making a wall chart.

■ Small group or class activity.

Return to the children's drawings of healthy and not so healthy people, and to the messages the children helped to write.

Invite the children to talk about what they think healthy people do and don't do. Note their answers. It is likely that these will focus on eating, drinking, taking exercise, dental care and fresh air. Encourage the children to think back to how healthy people *feel* (explored in Activity 1), to maintain their holistic view of healthy lifestyles.

Ask the children to help sort the activities they have suggested. Possible categories might be: eating and drinking, exercise, sleep, 'don'ts', keeping clean, teeth, fresh air, getting on with people, being happy.

The children could illustrate some of these activities and put their pictures into the different 'boxes' on a wall chart.

What do healthy people do?

eating and drinking	exercise	sleep
don'ts	keeping clean	teeth
fresh air	getting on with people	being happy

Return to what the children have contributed and talk about which of the activities healthy people do:

- all the time;

- some of the time;

- never.

This will provide opportunities to explore notions of 'every day', 'twice a day', 'regularly' and 'occasionally'.

Invite the children to contribute to a list beginning 'Healthy people don't...', and to give their explanations of *why* they don't. This will reveal much of the way children think and what they know, and will provide you with starting points for introducing new learning.

Activity 4 *Healthy messages*

- Making a 'healthy message' board.

- Class or group activity, with opportunity for family work.

Revise all the work relating to Content box 9, rereading the children's displayed drawings and writing.

Make, or draw, a 'healthy message' board. Recall the activities of healthy people, their healthy days and their messages. Invite the children to write and illustrate healthy messages to go on the board. Some ready-made banners and flags would be useful.

Family work: suggest to the children that they take home one of the message banners to fill in with the help of the family and display the banner at home or at school.

Our healthy messages

Don't smoke.

Wash your hands after you've been to the loo.

Learn to play safe.

Take care of yourself.

Keep yourself clean.

Activity 5 *What is a healthy day?*

■ Collecting and sorting pictures. Talking together.

■ Small group or pair activity.

Start a collection of pictures from magazines of people engaged in all types of healthy activity. They should illustrate hygiene, exercise, food, caring for others, the environment, keeping safe, being happy, resting, sleeping and relaxing.

Invite pairs or small groups of children to look through the pictures and arrange them to show a healthy day. Talk with the children about what they have included.

There are **cross-curricular links** with times of the day and telling the time.

Thomas and Suki made this healthy day for themselves.

sleeping   playing   crossing carefully   doing PE at school

drinking milk   getting washed   walking the dog   helping at home   cleaning teeth

Healthy lifestyles

Key words

survey   discover   analyse   results   display   differences   contract   target

Content box 7

> **7**
>
> *What do I think I do to make and keep myself healthy? What else do I need to know about being healthy? What is a healthy day for me?*

Activity 1 — *What do I think I do to make and keep myself healthy?*

■ Talking together. Explaining 'healthy'.

■ Class or group activity with individual starting points.

This would be a good time to use the 'Draw and write' technique (see Introduction and Appendix 1, page 231) which asks children to draw and label all those things they do, or think they do, to make and keep themselves healthy and to say who is responsible for keeping them healthy.

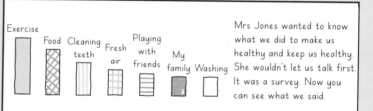

You could analyse the responses, inviting the children to help, setting out the results pictorially.

Activity 2 — *What else do I need to know?*

■ Talking together. Making a 'finding out' board. Literature.

■ Group and individual activity.

Some children may be ready to explore the ways in which their bodies work in a more scientific way, others will be ready to

explore relationships more fully. Using a 'finding out' board and special collections of books can motivate these new moves and provide opportunities for extending early study skills.

Activity 3) *What is a healthy day for me?*

■ Talking together. Drawing and writing.

■ Class, group or individual activity.

Invite the children to talk about their days, looking at what they do to make and keep themselves healthy. Look at similarities and differences. There are opportunities here to learn about each other's lifestyles.

Ask the children to illustrate and label, or write about, different aspects of their healthy days.

There are **cross-curricular links** with understanding time and telling the time.

> ### Healthy day words
>
> in the morning   in PE
> at playtime   when I get home
> before school   I choose
> at dinner time   I clean I help

Activity 4) *How healthy is my day?*

■ Revision. Talking together. Drawing and writing.

■ Class, group and individual activity, with opportunity for family work.

Revise the previous work on health related activities and healthy days.

Provide the children with a framework to fill in (see illustration below), or ask them to prepare it for themselves. Talk through each of the following steps with the children:

– this is me keeping healthy;

– this is what I need to do more often;

– this is what I need to do less often;

– these are the people who help to keep me healthy.

Ask the children to complete each step with drawings and writing.

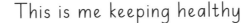

This is me keeping healthy

sleeping   eating    running   washing

This is what I think I need to do more often

help my mum   clean my teeth   wash my hands

Remind the children of all the people they have said help to keep them healthy. Did they include themselves? How do they help to keep themselves healthy?

Family work: this might be an opportunity for a group to devise a simple contract and to involve home and family.

CONTRACT

I am going to try ....

I am going to ask ....

.... to help me.

Signed ....

Remind the children that everyone has a right to health care, such as from doctors, nurses, hospitals, but that we all have our part to play.

Healthy lifestyles

Content box 26

26

*What do I think makes places
healthy or not so healthy?*

Activity 1 *What makes places healthy or not so healthy?*

- Talking together. Making a wall story.

- Class or group activity.

Invite the children to think whether places, like people, can be healthy.
How does a healthy place look? For example a school.

Make a note of the children's responses and use them to make a wall story
listing the characteristics of a healthy school. What do the responses focus
on? Encourage children to explain:

- how these characteristics make a school healthy;

- how much the happiness of a school matters to its health.

Talk with the children about whose job it is to make and keep the school
healthy. How can the children themselves make the job easier or harder?

A healthy school

clean, not smelly
warm, cool, happy
has nice dinners
soap in the toilet
good lessons   lots of PE
no bullies, nice people, places to play   someone to make you better
you can stay in when it's cold, nobody smokes, people keep the rules

These characteristics could be used by the children to look at their own
classroom, school building and playground in a different way, and to
decide what they themselves could do to help or improve things.

Can they help to make some 'healthy playground' rules? Talk with the children about the school's policies on litter, playground behaviour and bullying.

There are **cross-curricular links** with:

- topic work (especially on the environment or 'People who help us');

- visits and visitors;

- role-play;

- home and family.

Reflection and action

Look back with the children at all they have learned about different healthy ways and days.
- Remind them that they have made a contract to try to make their days more healthy, and warn them that keeping a contract isn't always easy. Suggest that they and you review progress.
- Remind them of all they said about schools needing to be healthy places and of all they can do to ensure that their school is a happy, healthy place.
- Ask them to practise this in the weeks ahead.

Key theme 2: Healthy eating

3

What do I eat? What do I like to eat and drink? Why do I eat? What meals do people eat? When? Where? Who tells me what to eat and drink? When can I choose for myself? What helps me to choose? What helps me to stick to my choice or to change my mind? For example TV, friends, learning about food.

34

Who keeps food clean and safe? What can I do to help?

23

What makes some of my days special? For example good experiences, happenings, surprises, food. What are the days I remember and the days I look forward to? For example happy times, sad times, landmarks.

These content boxes are from the Action Planners on pages 100, 101 and 102.

Focus of teaching
- Recognising the importance of food and meals in people's lifestyles and cultures, and the need for good hygiene in handling food.
- Awareness of the role of a balanced diet in their growth and vitality levels.
- Early understanding of the long-term outcomes of healthy eating.
- Understanding that foods cannot be labelled as 'good' or 'bad' for you.
- Heightened awareness of the amount and kind of food they eat in one day and the balance between snacks or treats and meals.
- Understanding that we all need to limit our intake of sugar, sugary drinks, fat and salt and to increase our intake of fruit, vegetables, cereals and breads, but that this is not easy to do.
- Recognising that, though they do not always have choices, there are ways in which they can choose, and that this is a new area of personal responsibility for them.
- Recognising that there are people in the community whose job it is to keep our food safe and healthy.

Key skills and competencies
Listening, speaking, discussion; recording and analysing views; categorising through criteria; reflecting; vocabulary of past, present, future; describing occasions and situations; making choices and decisions.

Citizenship opportunities
Opportunities for: participation in celebrations of people in all cultures; visits to places where rules about food hygiene are critical; visits to shops, stores, markets.

Links with children's literature
Stories about characters who eat too little, too much, or an unsuitable diet. Stories about characters who make decisions and stick to them. Stories about farm life and animals. Stories about family celebrations in different cultures.

Healthy eating

Content box 3

> What do I eat? What do I like to eat and drink? Why do I eat? What meals do people eat? When? Where? Who tells me what to eat and drink? When can I choose for myself? What helps me to choose? What helps me to stick to my choice or to change my mind? For example TV, friends, learning about food.

Activity 1 *What healthy eating means to me*

- Talking together. Drawing, writing and making a chart.

- Class, group and individual activity.

Invite the children to draw a picture of themselves feeling hungry. Collect words which describe the feeling of hunger, for example 'pain in the tummy', 'weak' and 'grumpy'.

Which foods and drinks make us healthy?			
fruit	vegetables	milk	eggs or cheese
✓ ✓ ✓ ✓ ✓ ✓ ✓ ✓ ✓ ✓	✓ ✓ ✓ ✓ ✓ ✓ ✓ ✓ ✓ ✓ ✓ ✓	✓ ✓ ✓ ✓	✓ ✓ ✓ ✓ ✓ ✓
10 of us said fruit	12 of us said vegetables	4 of us said milk	6 of us said eggs or cheese

Ask the children to draw and label the foods and drinks they think keep them healthy. Ask them to help you present their views as a chart (see illustration above) which shows the number of times each food is mentioned in their work.

Explore with the children what they think it is *about* these foods or *in* these foods that makes them healthy. It is important to discover how children explain this before starting to provide them with new information. Many children may respond in a general way with 'it's good things in them' and this can provide a starting point for teaching. It is very important to avoid the use of labels such as 'foods which are good for us' or 'foods which are bad for us' and to distinguish between 'health foods' and healthy foods.

Activity 2 | *Why do I eat and what do I eat?*

■ Talking together. Writing and drawing.

■ Class or group activity, with opportunity for individual work.

Talk with the children about the reasons why they eat.

Children's own explanations of why they eat are very illuminating and provide starting points for the wider exploration of the physical and social aspects of food.

Alternatively, ask the children to explain, in drawing and writing, why they eat, and then share their ideas with the rest of the group.

With the children make a list of foods which they like. Talk with them about why they like these foods. You may get a range of answers, for example:

– because I like the taste;

– they're grown up;

– they're special;

– we go out to eat them;

– My mum likes them.

This activity provides opportunities to talk about other people's foods and food traditions and to help the children become more aware of differences in lifestyles, as well as differences in healthy lifestyles.

Activity 3 | *When and where do we eat?*

■ Talking together. Making a wall story, collages and class or group books.

■ Class or group activity, with opportunity for individual and family work.

Ask the children to build up a list of names for the meals they eat during the day. Explore with the children the time of day and the occasions when these meals are eaten.

How are sweets referred to? For example 'treats'. Do they have more snacks and 'treats' or more meals?

Explore with the children where they eat and with whom. Ask them to find pictures in magazines which illustrate this and, individually or in groups, make them into collages.

Some groups could go on to explore who provides the food, who prepares it, who clears it away and who tells them to eat it.

Talk about the meaning of the word 'breakfast' and the importance of this meal after a night without food.

Family work: children could make their own books, incorporating all these ideas and take them home to share with their families, inviting them to make contributions.

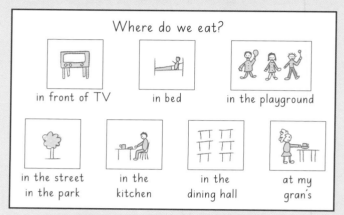

Where do we eat?

in front of TV   in bed   in the playground

in the street   in the   in the   at my
in the park   kitchen   dining hall   gran's

Activity 4 *Choosing for myself*

■ Talking together. Sorting ideas.

■ Class or group activity.

Opportunities for children in this age range to choose for themselves may be limited, but children will recognise times when they can influence food choices.

Talk with the children about a meal they have eaten recently. Who told them to eat it? What did this person say?

Eat it up quickly.
my dad

Eat it all up and then you can have seconds.
the midday helper

It will give you energy.
the lady on TV

my brother he wanted it

my tummy it grumbled

It will make you big and have strong bones and teeth.
the doctor

116

Talk about times when the children think they have had some choice:

– at school;

– at home;

– in the shop;

– in the café and take-away shop;

– for packed lunch.

Talk about choosing 'foods which make you healthy' in these situations. Ask them to look out for more opportunities to choose them.

There are opportunities to:

– encourage a positive approach to healthy eating and introduce early ideas on limiting the fat, sugar and salt in our diets and increasing cereals, fruit and vegetables;

– encourage a greater awareness of other people's lifestyles, special occasions and celebrations;

– introduce early survey and pictorial representation skills;

– use classroom play, setting up 'shops' and cafés', exploring themes about buying, preparing and cooking food, sharing meals and celebrating;

– use home links and **family work**.

Healthy eating

Key words

hygiene   disease   prevent   advice   rules   laws   responsibility

Content box 34

34

Who keeps food clean and safe? What can I do to help?

Activity 1 *Where does my food come from?*

- Talking together. Mapping information.

- Group or class activity.

This is a useful starting point for exploring many aspects of healthy eating. Here it is used to help the children focus on food hygiene.

Where does my food come from?

the market   the shops   the kitchen   another country where it's hot

a factory   the chip shop

the garden   the sea   the farm   the baker

in vans   on aeroplanes   on ships   in my dad's trolley

Invite the children to talk about where their food comes from, how it travels and how many people handle it. Make a simple map or diagram to illustrate this, representing distance in some way.

Ask the children to suggest ways in which food can be made to stay fresh and clean, and reasons why it might spoil.

Focus on day-to-day aspects of food hygiene, in particular children washing their hands before handling food, after playing (especially with pets) and after using the lavatory.

There are opportunities to talk about flies and the spreading of disease.

This would be a good time to introduce the differences between good advice, rules at home and school, and laws relating to food hygiene.

There are **cross-curricular links** with:

- topic work;
- visits and visitors;
- creative activities such as painting and model-making (appropriate for exploring the sources of foods).

There are opportunities to begin looking at the lifestyles of a range of people involved in the production, transport and hygiene of food, and the laws regarding the safe handling and preparation of food.

Healthy eating

Content box 23

> **23**
>
> *What makes some of my days special? For example good experiences, happenings, surprises, food. What are the days I remember and the days I look forward to? For example happy times, sad times, landmarks.*

Activity 1 *Our special days*

- Talking together. Role-play. Writing, drawing, painting and collecting pictures.

- Shared and individual activity, with opportunity for family work.

Many special occasions, landmarks and memories are linked with food, and by exploring them you can teach children more about eating for health.

Talk with the children about a recent special occasion, either a shared one, or one in which only some of the children were involved. Ask them to describe the foods which were part of the occasion. Write down and read through the children's responses. This could be an opportunity to use role-play.

Invite the children, as a group, to describe the special nature of the preparation and eating of food on special occasions. Invite them to choose illustrations of food which have been drawn, painted or cut from magazines, and to label or write about them.

Family work: this would be an opportunity to involve parents and people in the community.

Special day foods

Pancakes   special sweets   birthday cake

rice   wedding cake   samosas

Easter eggs   no food   squash

■ Writing and drawing. Talking together.

■ Individual and group activity.

Ask the children to make individual versions of the shared writing and drawing from Activity 1.

Talk with the group about different kinds of special days. Which ones can they remember? Include both good and not so good days. Was food part of the celebration? Was food comforting on a sad occasion?

There are **cross-curricular links** with:

– history, geography and literature;

– learning about and valuing other cultures and traditions;

– making visits and inviting visitors to the school;

– cooking and/or tasting a wide variety of foods eaten on special occasions.

Reflection and action

Look back with the children at all they have learned about eating healthily.

• Ask them to practise thinking about their days and improving the balance between the foods which are 'treats' and those which they need for growth, energy and good health.

Key theme 3:
Feelings and relationships

14

What makes me the same as you? What are the feelings we all share? For example being happy, sad, cheerful, afraid, uneasy, shy, clumsy. What makes us different? How does it feel to be different?

20

What makes me feel good about myself and my days? How do I feel when I feel good? What can I do to help make myself feel good?

36

Who are our special people and friends? What do they do and say? What do we do together? What do we share or keep secret? What do I like about them and like doing with them? What makes me scared sometimes or uneasy? Who can I tell?

These content boxes are from the Action Planners on pages 100, 101 and 102.

Focus of teaching
- Extending the ability to empathise with other people's feelings and concerns and to demonstrate this in their behaviour toward the person.
- Extending understanding of tolerance and valuing other people's lives and beliefs, and putting this into practice.
- Recognising that each of us is unique and special and always treating ourselves and others as such.
- Understanding that they are part of many groups and networks which are different and similar in many ways.
- Understanding that there is a whole range of what people may call 'secrets', some of which are easily shared, some related to threats and fears.
- Understanding the importance of finding and telling someone if they feel threatened, bullied or ill-treated, physically or in other ways.

Key skills and competencies
Listening, speaking, discussion; language of feelings and emotions (adjectives); self-esteem; working individually, in pairs, in groups; comparing, contrasting; word pictures of different experiences; self-description; role-play.

Citizenship opportunities
Opportunities for: visits to a wide range of people – old, with special needs; visits from those agencies in the community which help with their problems.

Links with children's literature
Stories about characters with fears and problems: the dark, new places, new situations. Stories about characters who found someone to tell and help.

Feelings and relationships

Key words

feelings	problems	similar	different	special	share	unique

Content box 14

> What makes me the same as you? What are the feelings we all share? For example being happy, sad, cheerful, afraid, uneasy, shy, clumsy. What makes us different? How does it feel to be different?

Activity 1 *What makes me the same as you?*

■ Drawing and painting. Talking together. Making a class book.

■ Individual and small group activity.

Invite the children to draw or paint a portrait of themselves. Display these (without names), asking children to identify themselves and each other if possible. You could contribute a portrait too.

Talk about the portraits and the people they represent. Invite the children to share in making a list of all the ways in which the people in the class are the same. A useful starter might be: 'We are all in the same class'.

Encourage the children to think about the physical attributes they all share, and to widen their thinking and look at activities which are liked by the whole class, for example PE or story time.

Suggest the children think about feelings which they all share at some time or other, for example love, hate, happiness, sadness, worry, excitement, tiredness, being full of energy.

Children could contribute individual items to a group book entitled 'We are all the same'.

We are all the same

We are happy.   We are sad.   We are worried.

Activity 2 *What feelings do we all share?*

■ Talking together and making a 'circle of feelings'. Drawing and writing.

■ Small group activity.

Invite the children to help make a 'circle of feelings' (making a circle rather than a list ensures that none are prioritised). Start them off by providing one or two examples, if necessary.

Invite the children to share with each other, through talking, drawing and writing, the times when they have experienced one or more of these feelings. You could share your own experiences with them too.

There are **cross-curricular links** with:

– movement, drama and role-play;

– literature.

You could link this with other opportunities for talking with children about particular problems, such as at circle time.

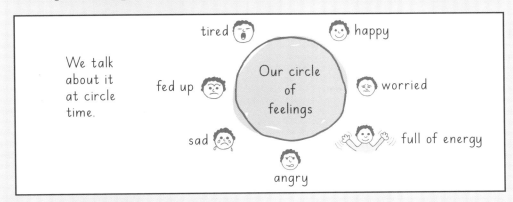

Activity 3 *What makes us different?*

■ Role-play. Talking together.

■ Class or group activity.

Describe a situation to the children, for example:

– a spider climbing on you;

– being left out or not chosen to play with the others;

– breaking something precious;

– losing something important.

Act out these situations using role-play. Ask the children to talk about how they reacted. Did they all feel the same and do the same thing?

This is me, Naomi.
I am special.
There isn't another me.

I am tall.
I am a bit
clumsy sometimes.
I am happy when
I play with my friend.
I am angry if he wins.

I am unique.

Recall Activity 1: 'What makes me the same as you?' Talk about what makes us different, for example feelings, shape, colour, being the youngest or the oldest.

Emphasise how special it is 'being me', being unique, finding out the special things about 'being me' and valuing these.

It is possible to extend this activity to look at differences in where the children live, how they come to school, the pets they have and their interests. Whichever topic is explored it is important that the children come back to the original theme: that we are in many ways alike, but that each of us is unique and special.

Activity 4   *How does it feel to be different?*

- Talking together. Stories and poems.

- Group and individual activity.

This aspect of feelings and relationships can be approached in many ways. One way is to approach it through a story or poem about someone, or something, being or feeling very different from others, for example *The Ugly Duckling*.

Invite the children to talk about how such a character might have felt at different times in the story. Was being different a good, or not so good, feeling?

The Ugly Duckling   He thought no   It made him very sad.
knew he was different.   one liked him.   It wasn't a good feeling.

Who made him feel better?

Glen

The other swans did.
He did.
He found he was beautiful.

Feelings and relationships

Key words

good   not so good   great   conquered   confident   brave   help   understand

Content box 20

20

What makes me feel good about myself and my days? How do I feel when I feel good? What can I do to help make myself feel good?

Activity 1 *Feeling good about my days*

- Talking together. Writing, drawing and making a class or group book.

- Class or group activity, with opportunity for individual work.

Invite the children to draw or describe a picture of a 'feeling good' day, one where they felt good about what they had done or about what had happened. Invite them to share with others, through talking or writing, what made it a good day. Help the children write down their ideas, perhaps as the first stage in making a class or group book.

Explore with them the idea of feeling good about oneself and one's day.

125

Activity 2 *Feeling good about myself*

- Talking together. Drawing. Making a 'circle of feelings'.

- Individual and shared activity.

Explore further with the children the different kinds of activities which make people feel good, for example learning a new skill, doing something better than before, helping someone else, making new friends, being more confident and conquering fear.

Invite the children to draw pictures of themselves feeling good. Talk about the feeling and how it is reflected in facial expressions and body language. Talk about how we recognise people feeling good about themselves.

Ask the children to recall some words for feeling good. Collect them into a 'circle of feelings'. Read and reread this, exploring the facial expressions and body language to go with the words.

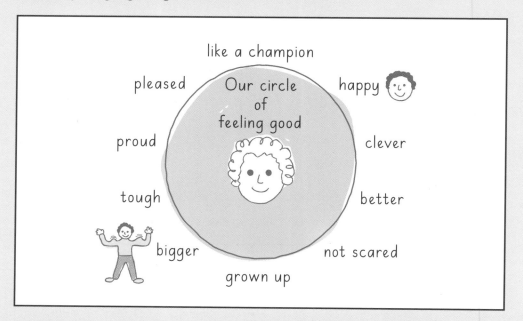

Ask the children to think of things they can do to help make themselves feel good, for example:

- ask someone to join in;

- practise and get better at things;

- help people and share;

- be happy and not worry;

- tell people when we are worried;

- feel special all day;

- keep healthy and happy.

Make a new collection of words and phrases for feeling good.

There are **cross-curricular links** with:

- physical education;

- literature;

- music;

- creative activities;

- role-play;

- drama;

- religious education.

Feelings and relationships

Key words

special   comfortable   worried   rules   safe   dangerous   real   imaginary   pretend

Content box 36

> **36**
>
> *Who are our special people and friends? What do they do and say? What do we do together? What do we share or keep secret? What do I like about them and like doing with them? What makes me scared sometimes or uneasy? Who can I tell?*

Activity 1 *People who are special to me*

- Drawing and writing. Talking together. Making a class or group collage or individual books.

- Individual and group activity.

Invite the children to draw or describe some of the people who are special to them. Invite them to share, through talking or writing, what it is that makes each person special. Is it what they do? or say? or feel?

Children will respond with a wide range of suggestions, for example family and friends, and explanations about being special.

An interesting activity would be to collect their drawings and written explanations and make them into a collage entitled 'These are our special people'. Alternatively, the children could make their own books, in small groups or individually.

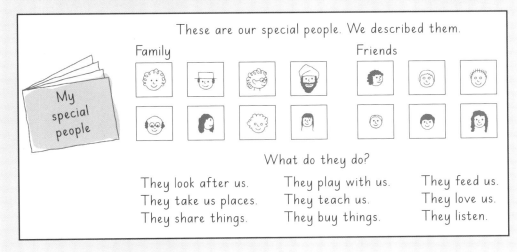

These are our special people. We described them.

Family   Friends

My special people

What do they do?

They look after us.   They play with us.   They feed us.
They take us places.   They teach us.   They love us.
They share things.   They buy things.   They listen.

Our special people

Who are they? What do we like to do with them?

sit with them in school

visit them

share secrets

go out with them

stay in their houses

have a cuddle

play tricks on them

play a game with them

go swimming with them

have fun

give them things

swap things

talk to them when we are upset

Talk about the things the children do which make their special people happy, pleased, worried and angry, and why this is so. There will be opportunities here to develop some basic ideas on keeping safe, good relationships and awareness of the impact of one's actions on other people. You could also talk about some rules for keeping safe:

- saying where you are going;

- saying 'No', even if it seems to upset people;

- sometimes not keeping secrets.

There are **cross-curricular links** with:

- literature;

- role-play.

Activity 2 *What makes me scared or uneasy?*

■ Talking together. Stories and poems. Making a 'circle of feelings' and a chart. Role-play.

■ Small group and pair activity, with opportunity for family work.

Recall with the children the previous work on special people and what they enjoy doing for and with them. Remind the children that some of their special people can help them when there is a problem or when they are afraid.

You could use a poem or story in which fear is overcome or where a child character admits to fear and tells a special person.

Talk with the children about real fears and hazards in comparison with pretend or imaginary ones, for example 'monsters'. You could share some of your own fears, both real and imaginary, with them.

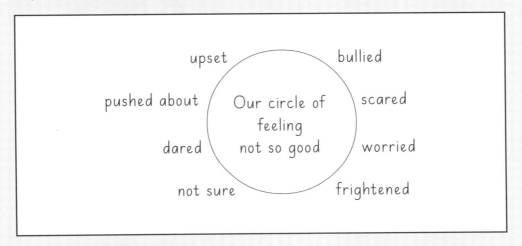

Ask the children to recall some words for feeling not so good. Collect them into a 'circle of feelings' and explore the facial expressions, gestures and body language that go with the words. Talk with the children about *when* they feel this way and write their responses on a chart.

You will know whether it is likely that the children will respond with statements similar to those in the illustration or whether it would be appropriate to ask 'What if ...'.

Role-play one or more of the situations suggested by the children and invite them to try out different ways in which the problem could be resolved. What could they say or do? Who could they ask for help? How would they ask for help or tell someone?

Invite the children to work in pairs to practise these strategies. Offer some phrases they could start with, for example 'Please listen', 'I want to tell you something', 'I'm worried and scared about something, will you listen?'

Family work: take the opportunities which arise when planning and exploring these themes to negotiate with, and enlist support from, the children's families and the community.

Reflection and action

Look back with the children at all they have learned.
- Remind them to think back over their days and pick out all the special things which have happened to them and around them.
- Ask them to help other people find their days special in some way.
- Remind them to practise making people listen to them when they are worried or have problems, and to share their feelings, the good and the not so good, with their special people.

Ages 6 and 7

Sensitive Issues

Key themes

Key theme 1:
The world of drugs

This section describes in detail further classroom strategies and activities to develop the work done previously on the theme of drugs.

The five content boxes on page 133 each have a distinctive focus and act as starting points for the classroom activities set out in this section. You will find that the questions in each content box stimulate discussion, and help you to build on previous skills and knowledge and to identify where the children are in their understanding.

It is important that you select and extend the classroom activities according to: your PSHE or PSD and Citizenship programmes; your Healthy School initiatives; the school's Drug Education Policy; and involve the support of the children's families, the school governors and the local community.

Focus of teaching

- Extending understanding of what goes into their bodies, how it enters and its impact.
- Categorising what goes into their bodies in different ways, including safe, dangerous, legal and illegal.
- Extending their understanding of the rules of medicines to include other substances.
- Introducing the rules for finding syringes and needles.
- Understanding that some people need drugs all through their lives to maintain health.
- Understanding that medicines can make their bodies better but do this by learning what makes them feel good about themselves.

Key skills and competencies

Wider discussion and communication skills; more demanding group skills; categorising knowledge and views according to given criteria; sharing views; making word pictures; extending language of feelings; rule making and extending.

Citizenship opportunities

Opportunities for: introducing children to the laws (of illegal drugs) which are set up to protect them; rule making and keeping; learning about the work of non-government groups; working with Environmental Health Officers.

Links with children's literature

Stories where characters learn about staying within the rules of the place, the game or the situation. Stories about people feeling not so good about themselves and learning to be confident of their skills. Stories where characters, in particular from the animal world, find 'medical' advice and cures.

The world of drugs

1

What goes into my body?
Can I name these things? Do other people have different names for them? How do they get in? Who puts them there? Who tells me to put them into my body? What is the difference between 'accidently' and 'on purpose'? Which things are safe, not so safe, dangerous, legal and illegal? When should I say 'No, don't' and 'I'll ask someone'? How do all these different things feel, smell and taste as they go into my body? What do I say? do? think? Do I like it or not? Do I feel worried or unsure?

2

Where do things go when they enter my body?
Where do things go when they enter through my mouth? through my nose? through my skin? What does my body do with the good, not so good and the dangerous things so I will stay healthy? How can I help to keep myself healthy? What should I do when people tell me to try (touch, taste, sniff or puff) things? How do I know who to trust? How best can I say 'No, I won't' and 'I'll ask someone'? Who are the people I can ask? tell? talk to?

3

Injections
When and why do I have injections? For example: to prevent me from becoming ill later on; before I visit another country; in an emergency; an accident; at the dentist; at the hospital; so it doesn't hurt so much; to extract some of my blood. What are the rules about finding syringes and needles? How can I find and tell a safe person?

4

Feeling ill and feeling better
How do I feel when I'm ill? How do I look and sound? What can I and can't I do? Who and what helps me to get well? How can I help myself and other people? What kinds of drugs which are medicines help us to get well? Who decides whether I need to swallow or sniff them, or have injections? Can I remember the 'medicine wise' rules? Are there some new ones to learn? Can I be a good example? How do I feel when I'm getting better? How do I help myself?

5

How can I feel good about myself without using medicines or drugs?
What makes me feel good about myself? not so good? What makes me feel better? What can I do? Is this a new kind of medicine?

Key messages

for learning to live in a drug-using world

Learn:

- that all medicines are drugs but not all drugs are medicines;

- what goes onto and into your body;

- what happens to things when they enter your body;

- when and how to say 'No, I won't', 'I'll ask', 'It's OK'. Practise this;

- about the places where medicines, drugs, dangerous and strange things might be found;

- where and how medicines can be obtained;

- to describe and talk about your feelings to people you trust;

- which people you can trust.

Understand:

- that you can feel good and feel better without taking medicines or using drugs;

- that cigarettes and alcohol have drugs in them;

- when people or friends are trying to persuade you to try (touch, taste, sniff or puff) strange substances;

- that some people need drugs which are medicines to live a normal life or to get well;

- that some drugs prevent us from contracting some diseases;

- that some drugs are illegal.

Practise:

- keeping the rules about medicines, drugs, syringes and needles;

- explaining the rules to other children and setting a good example to younger ones.

Share these key messages with parents, families and people in the community so that they can support and reinforce them.

The world of drugs

Key words

swallowed   absorbed   injected   legal   illegal   persuaded   refuse   tell

Content box 1

What goes into my body?

Can I name these things? Do other people have different names for them? How do they get in? Who puts them there? Who tells me to put them into my body? What is the difference between 'accidently' and 'on purpose'? Which things are safe, not so safe, dangerous, legal and illegal? When should I say 'No, don't' and 'I'll ask someone'? How do all these different things feel, smell and taste as they go into my body? What do I say? do? think? Do I like it or not? Do I feel worried or unsure?

Activity 1 *What goes into my body?*

■ Talking together. Drawing and writing. Making a display. Categorising.

■ Individual and class or group activity.

Ask the children to think of all the things which can get into their bodies, to draw some of these things and to label them.

The children could pool their ideas in groups or as a class and display their pictures. Have they included things such as splinters, thorns, food, drink, medicines, pills? What about the less obvious things such as air, cigarette smoke, sunlight, germs, dirt, foreign bodies? Have they included sprays such as those used by children suffering from asthma?

Talk with the children about the different ways these things can get into their bodies, for example by being swallowed, injected, sniffed, rubbed in or absorbed via a cut or broken skin. Look with the class at how their suggestions fit into these categories. Can they find any new categories, for example, up my nose, down my throat?

Look at different ways of categorising, for example:

– I chose it – I was hungry;

– accidentally – I didn't mean to, I fell over;

– someone told me to – persuaded me;

– it's there and I can't stop it going in.

Activity 2 *Which things are safe?*

■ Talking together. Categorising. Making a chart.

■ Class activity, with opportunity for individual and group work.

Look again at the children's work from Activity 1. Review how, when and why some of these things would be dangerous. Offer the children some possible categories to help them sort their suggestions.

We think these are safe:	We think these could be dangerous:	We know these are dangerous:
breakfast dinner	dirt splinters	
tea perfume	other people's medicines	medicines the doctor didn't give you
some things you buy at school	things you sniff	
	pollution sunshine	drugs
sweets crisps	things pushed up your nose	pills cigarettes

You could make this into a chart which the children could illustrate and add to. Ask the children to give their reasons for including items in these categories. This could be an opportunity in Citizenship to introduce the notions of legal and illegal, and to remind them that it is illegal to sell alcohol and cigarettes to children.

Reinforce children's understanding that in some cases, it is not the objects that are harmful, but the way they behave with these objects.

Activity 3 *What do I say if someone tries to persuade me?*

■ Talking together. Drawing. Making a display.

■ Class, group and individual activity, with opportunity for family work.

Invite the children to talk about and illustrate in the same way a situation when someone is trying to persuade them to try (touch, taste, sniff or puff) something dangerous or unknown. What can they say when they are worried, under pressure or unsure? Practise some ways of refusing.

Make a note of the children's responses and display them. Help the children to practise them, where possible using their own words. Reassure children that telling an adult in these circumstances is a sensible way of behaving.

Family work: encourage the children to explain their work to their families and enlist their help and support.

There are **cross-curricular links** with: science; personal safety education.

The world of drugs

Content box 2

> **2**
>
> **Where do things go when they enter my body?**
> *Where do things go when they enter through my mouth? through my nose? through my skin? What does my body do with the good, not so good and the dangerous things so I will stay healthy? How can I help to keep myself healthy? What should I do when people tell me to try (touch, taste, sniff or puff) things? How do I know who to trust? How best can I say 'No, I won't' and 'I'll ask someone'? Who are the people I can ask? tell? talk to?*

Activity 1 *Where do things go when they enter my body?*

■ Talking together. Drawing and writing. Making a display.

■ Individual, class and pair or group activity.

Remind the children of their previous work on the items which enter their bodies and how they get in. Without further discussion, invite them to draw what they think is inside their bodies.

Ask the children to use coloured pencils to show:

– how food and air get in and where they go;

– how germs from a cut get in and where they go;

– how sunshine gets in and where it goes.

Invite the children to share their ideas with a partner, or in a small group, before coming together as a larger group to pool their ideas and display their pictures.

Investigate in a similar way how the children think their bodies deal with the good and the not so good items which are taken in. You are likely to receive responses such as:

- my body uses the good bits;

- it gives me tummy ache;

- it makes me sick;

- my body fights the germs.

- my body gets rid of the bad bits;

- it makes me cough;

- it makes me feel sleepy;

Children can be asked to illustrate, label and expand on their responses. Once you are aware of the children's perceptions you will be able to see which, and how much, new scientific information is relevant and appropriate.

Some children's concepts of their body systems may be well advanced and they will be ready for a more scientific approach; other children might find such an approach confusing and need more activities.

Activity 2 *How can I help to keep myself healthy?*

- Talking together. Drawing. Sharing views.

- Class or group activity, with opportunity for individual work.

Remind the children that there are a lot of people who help to keep them healthy and safe from harmful things going into their bodies. Who are these people? Collect up the children's ideas.

These people help me to keep healthy and safe from harmful things getting into my body

mum	dad	nurse	doctor
teacher	clean air people		police
good friends		chemist	
clean water people		ME !	

Ask the children to make a class list of all the things *they* do to help all these people do their 'keeping us healthy' jobs. Remind them that their contribution is the most important.

Helping my body keep healthy

tell   ask

get first aid   be responsible

eat healthy foods   not try dangerous things

not touch cigarettes   not sniff things

get lots of sun and fresh air   don't listen to stupid people

feel good   keep clean

Ask the children to think about people who might try to persuade them to try (touch, taste, sniff or puff) strange substances. Who are these people? Ask the children to illustrate and talk about people who might try to persuade them. Look at the children's pictures for stereotyping of strangers or dangerous people.

Encourage the children to think about what such people might *say*, rather than what they look like. Write in speech bubbles what the children think these people might say (for example 'They are only like sweets' or 'It won't hurt') and how they themselves might answer them (for example 'It's dangerous' or 'No, I won't'). Help them to practise listening to persuasion and then making confident refusals. You can also help them to practise telling an adult that they are being persuaded to take something. This is an important coping strategy. Talk with the children about the people who they feel they can trust. Invite them to illustrate and label these people. Explore, where possible, individual children's choices and reasons for trust.

There are **cross-curricular links** with:

- personal safety education;

- topics on the home and local community.

The world of drugs

Content box 3

> **3**
>
> *Injections*
> *When and why do I have injections? For example: to prevent me from becoming ill later on; before I visit another country; in an emergency; an accident; at the dentist; at the hospital; so it doesn't hurt so much; to extract some of my blood. What are the rules about finding syringes and needles? How can I find and tell a safe person?*

Activity 1 *When and why do I have injections?*

- Talking together, drawing and writing. Collecting pictures.

- Class or group activity.

Ask the children to talk, illustrate and write (or dictate) about the times when they, or someone they know, had to have injections, blood tests or transfusions. Some children might have experienced a situation when a dog or cat had to have an injection, and this could also provide a useful starting point. Encourage the children to include injections for vaccinations, emergencies, dental treatment, hospital treatment and blood tests.

Ask the children what they think is the purpose of an injection and how it makes them feel before and after the jab. Remind the children that the injection is a drug, doing the work of medicines, and that these drugs have to be accounted for and the syringes destroyed as soon as they have been used on one person.

Where appropriate, talk about people who need an injection daily (such as diabetics) and emphasise that injections can be used in a positive and controlled way. It would be valuable to involve the school nurse and parents at this stage, and to talk about your own experiences.

! Some children may be having or have had the experience of seeing adults using syringes with both legal and illegal substances. It is important that the lesson focuses on the positive aspects of injections and the safety precautions, and not specifically on the illegality.

Display the children's work and emphasise both how important these kinds of injections are to these people, and the careful way they should be handled.

Talk with the children about their reactions to injections. What did they do, say or think? Invite them to write what they said or thought on speech bubbles, and then glue them onto their own drawings or onto relevant pictures cut from magazines.

 Activity 2 *Whose job is it to give me injections?*

■ Talking together.

■ Class or group activity.

Ask the children to think of all the safe people whose job it is to use syringes and needles of this kind, for example doctors, nurses, dentists and vets. Talk about how they use syringes safely.

Remind the children of the rules about finding syringes. Explain that the needle in the end of the syringe:

> Be safe   Stay safe
>
> If you find a syringe:
> – leave it where it is
> – don't touch it
> – don't pick it up
> – find a grown up and
>   tell them
> – keep others away

– will have been inside someone or something else's body;

– will be sharp; and that even a scratch from the needle or a pin prick could be dangerous.

Ensure that your school has a policy and the necessary skill and equipment for dealing with needles and accidents.

 Activity 3 *Who do I tell? What do I say?*

■ Talking together. Making a shared picture. Making a poster. Role-play.

■ Class or group activity.

Ask the children to close their eyes and describe a safe person – someone they could tell and trust if they found a syringe.

Make a shared picture. How many children thought the person would wear a uniform? be a woman? Identify people in the community who would be safe people.

This could be an opportunity to involve local members of the community, especially those who are there on a regular basis, for example shopkeepers. The children could make a 'safe person, safe place' poster to go up in the shop windows, and rehearse asking for help.

There are **cross-curricular links** with:

– science;   – topic work;   – safety education.

The world of drugs

Content box 4

4

Feeling ill and feeling better
How do I feel when I'm ill?
How do I look and sound?
What can I and can't I do?
Who and what helps me to get well? How can I help myself and other people?
What kinds of drugs which are medicines help us to get well? Who decides whether I need to swallow or sniff them, or have injections? Can I remember the 'medicine wise' rules? Are there some new ones to learn? Can I be a good example? How do I feel when I'm getting better? How do I help myself?

Activity 1 *How do I feel?*

■ Talking together. Categorising. Making a display.

■ Class or group activity, with opportunity for family work.

Talk with the children about a time when they were ill. Collect up their memories of how they felt. Invite them to categorise these feelings into 'Feelings in my body' and 'Feelings about being ill'.

Remind the children that they can help themselves to feel and get better by:

– following the doctor's instructions;

– resting;

– taking medicines;

– looking forward to being better.

Ask the children what they could do to make someone they know who is ill feel better. Collect up and add to their ideas.

Making people feel better

Send them a   Take them   Visit them but don't
get well card.   a present.   stay too long.

Say you've had it   Promise them a
too and you soon   special treat when
got better.   they are better.

Ask the children to set up a 'Getting better' display showing some of these things. Add books and pictures.

Activity 2 *Feeling better*

- Using an imaginary situation. Talking together. Revision of 'medicine wise' rules.

- Class work, with opportunity for group work.

Ask the children to put themselves in this scenario:

'You have been ill and miserable because it has taken a long time to get better. Every day has been long and dull. You wake up one morning, sit up, and suddenly you know you are getting better.'

How do you know?

You know you are getting better because:

you've stopped itching   you want to get up

you are hungry   you want to get
dressed and go out

you feel good

Remind the children of who and what helped them to get better and how much they themselves helped.

Look back at the role of medicines, lotions, sprays, pills and injections in helping to make them better.

Ask the children to recall some words for feeling better. Collect them into a 'circle of feelings'.

What helped me feel better?

taking my medicine
staying in bed
my gran
taking a pill
hot water bottle
doing what I was told
present
not moaning
lots to drink
the doctor

full of energy
happy
super special
busting to go
hungry
Our circle of feeling better
lonely
lively
a bit wobbly
fed up with staying in

This would be a good opportunity to remind the children of the 'medicine wise' rules and the reasons behind them.

Revise rules about:

- taking only medicines prescribed for you;

- not trying other people's medicines;

- taking the correct dose and only when it is given by a safe person;

- not trying (touching, tasting, sniffing or puffing) anything unknown;

- recognising people who are trying to persuade you to try (touch, taste, sniff or puff) something, and saying 'No';

- remembering that younger children are not as well informed about medicines and drugs, and how important it is to make sure that all medicines are put away safely and that you set a good example;

- remembering that *all* medicines are drugs but not all drugs are medicines.

The world of drugs

Key words

medicine   drug   feeling good   not so good   better   problem   invent   relax
allergies   responsibility

Content box 5

> **5**
>
> **How can I feel good about myself without using medicines or drugs?**
> What makes me feel good about myself? not so good? What makes me feel better? What can I do? Is this a new kind of medicine?

Activity 1 *What can I do when I am feeling healthy, happy and well?*

■ Drawing. Talking together.

■ Class, group and individual activity.

Ask the children to draw a picture of themselves feeling good about themselves and full of health. Look at what they have drawn. How have they portrayed themselves? For example:

– with a smile?

– jumping about?

– playing with friends?

– running with the dog?

– relaxing?

Ask them to turn the paper over and draw a picture of themselves feeling not so good about themselves and not so healthy. How have they portrayed themselves?

Talk with the children about the things they can do, or do better, when they feel good about themselves. For example:

– exercise;

– have fun;

– play with friends;

– learn something new;

– work;

– help someone else;

– solve problems. (What kind of problem could they solve?)

Remind the children that there isn't a medicine which can make them feel better about themselves, so they will have to invent one.

Our 'feeling better about yourself' medicine

 talk to someone

 hug the dog

 help someone

 run about and shout

 do something on your own

Remind the children that this is a different kind of medicine but that it works well. Ask them to practise this new kind of medicine.

Remind the children that some people have to take medicines all their lives so that they stay healthy. Reinforce the fact that some children do have specific allergies or diets and help your class work positively in this too. You could ask the school nurse or members of different helping organisations to come and talk about these allergies and other problems.

This would be a good time to teach the class how to tell a member of the staff that a child is suffering from an attack of some kind in the playground.

Remind the children that they need to be able to describe what is happening, for example 'she's wheezing' rather than 'she's not very well'.

Reflection and action

Look back with the children at all they have learned.
- Remind the children that they have been looking at all the things which go into their bodies and learning to sort them into 'safe', 'could be dangerous' and 'dangerous'.
- Remind them that they have learned that alcohol and cigarettes are illegal for children, and that there are other dangerous drugs which are not medicines and which are illegal for anyone to use.
- Remind them that they have a part to play in getting better from an illness, and that feeling good about yourself is a great help.
- Rehearse the rules for what to do if they find a syringe or needle, and how to tell a safe adult.
- Remind them that STOP and THINK is a good rule.
- Remind them to share what they have learned with their families and to practise keeping these rules at home.

Key theme 2: Keeping myself safe

For this theme, it is important that you select and extend the classroom activities according to: your PSHE or PSD and Citizenship programmes; your Healthy School initiatives; Health and Safety regulations; child abuse procedures.

Focus of teaching
- Recognising that their views of what they have to keep safe from can be different from the views of people whose job it is to keep them safe.
- Widening understanding of real, imaginary and pretend.
- Recognising persuasion, particularly where secrets are involved.
- Exploring the outside world in terms of pleasure, hazards, dangers and risks, particularly routes to school, shops and play areas.
- Recognising the impact of their own feelings on their behaviour and on other people's.
- Recognising that their own and other people's feelings can be hurt, even if the hurt is not visible, and modifying their own behaviour accordingly.
- Knowing where they live, where they are going, who is in charge and when they themselves are in charge.
- Widening their understanding of accidents and their causes.
- Recognising the differences between advice rules and laws.
- Recognising and valuing people and organisations who work to keep children safe. Recognising that this also includes members of the public.
- Recognising their own growing responsibilities.

Key skills and competencies
Widening the language of feelings and valuing; listening, shared discussion; summarising shared views; coming to a consensus; clarifying differences in concepts of risk, accidents, behaviour, feelings; reflection; projection; rule making; mapping routes; describing people, places, situations; responsibilities.

Citizenship opportunities
Opportunities to: meet and learn something of the organisation of local and national services, government and voluntary organisations concerned with the wellbeing of young children and their personal safety; introduce First Aid and meet with those who organise training for young people; share their 'everywhere' rules with other children, with family and the community.

Links with children's literature
Stories about other people's working lives and lifestyles. Stories where characters: have an 'everywhere' rule; recognise or fail to recognise persuasion, pretence, pressure. Stories that widen the vocabulary of feelings.

Keeping myself safe

1

Focus on feelings
What do I feel I have to keep safe from? Are these real or pretend dangers? Which people and places are dangerous? Is it something I do that makes them dangerous? How do I keep myself safe? Do I have rules for different places? Is telling someone a good way of keeping safe? What makes me feel unsafe?
When am I most at risk?

4

Focus on outdoors
Where are the best places to play and explore? What makes these places safe, risky or dangerous? What makes them fun, exciting and interesting? What are the rules of these places? Can I remember them all? What am I getting better at? What can I learn to do so I'm safer in the street, by the water, etc? How can I learn more about being a road user?
When am I most at risk?

2

Focus on me
Who am I? Where do I live? Where am I going? Where have I been? Who am I with? Who have I been with? Who is in charge? What time is it? How late is it? How do I get there? How do I ask the way or ask for help? What do 'safe', 'dangerous' and 'risky' mean? What is good about being bigger and older? When is it risky? What can I do to help keep myself safe?
When am I most at risk?

3

Focus on indoors
What do I enjoy doing indoors? at home? at school? What can make play activities dangerous? What can make me safer? Is it something I can do? Who or what makes an accident happen? What are the rules indoors? Do the rules and risks depend on people and places? What am I getting better at? What would I like to be able to do? What does 'risky' mean?
When am I most at risk?

5

Focus on people
Who will help me to keep safe? How do I recognise people whose job it is to keep me safe? What are they trying to teach us to do, or not to do? How can I help them? How do I know who to ask for help? Who are the people who threaten my safety? How do I recognise them? How can I keep myself safe?
When am I most at risk?

Key messages
for keeping myself safe

Learn:

- who you are, where you live, who is at home, your telephone number, an alternative safe place to go;

- where you are, where you're supposed to be, who knows where you are, where you are going, where you've been, how to get out safely, the time, how long it takes to go from here to there;

- who can help you and what the limits of that help should be;

- about the day-to-day hazards where you live, play and go to school;

- about the safe places to play, how to play safely and the rules of different places;

- how to distinguish between the safe people and the not so safe people;

- how accidents can happen.

Understand:

- that you and your body are special, valuable and unique, and that some things which other people want you to do may not fit in with this;

- that you can say 'No', even if at the time it may seem rude or unkind;

- that there are real and pretend people, feelings, threats and promises;

- that telling people about your fears and worries and making them listen is not 'telling tales', but is a good way to get help;

- that getting told off is different from other dangers;

- that you can prevent accidents.

Practise:

- the skills which help you to keep safe in traffic, near water, in and around the home, with people and on your own;

- saying 'No', 'Stop', 'I'll ask';

- asking for help, making people listen and describing exactly what happened;

- keeping family rules and the rules of different places;

- doing things for yourself;

- playing safely, having fun and feeling safe.

Share these key messages with parents, families and people in the community so that they can support and reinforce them.

Keeping myself safe

Key words

real   pretend   imagination   breaking rules   laws   tell   dangerous
feelings   my responsibility

Content box 1

> **Focus on feelings**
> *What do I feel I have to keep safe from? Are these real or pretend dangers? Which people and places are dangerous? Is it something I do that makes them dangerous? How do I keep myself safe? Do I have rules for different places? Is telling someone a good way of keeping safe? What makes me feel unsafe?*
> **When am I most at risk?**

Activity 1 *What do I feel I have to keep safe from?*

■ Drawing and writing. Talking together. Categorising.

■ Class, group and individual activity.

Invite the children to think about the things they feel they have to keep safe from, and to draw and label as many of these as they can without discussion.

Ask them to pool their responses and categorise them under the headings: 'real things' and 'pretend things', or 'things', 'people' and 'places' (which can then be subdivided into 'real' and 'pretend').

We are keeping safe from

things	people	places
knives	bullies	the road
scissors	strangers	
kettle	people who bother you	the railway
hot fat		the river
monsters	vandals	

Explore with the children why they think these people, places and things are dangerous, asking: 'Can they hurt us or is it what we do?' 'Are there rules to help us?' Using this framework, children can begin to distinguish between hazards which they themselves can cause (for example by being in an unsafe place, by playing with things not intended for play, or by taking risks) and hazards which are caused by other people not taking care, or other people who do things to them (for example bullying or abuse).

Activity 2 *How do I keep myself safe?*

- Talking together. Classroom play. Making a 'circle of feelings'. Role-play or mime.

- Class or group activity.

Invite the children to review their list of things, people and places which they keep safe from. Ask them how they think they keep safe in different places and situations, and make a note of these.

Look at how many of the children's strategies are 'Do's' and how many are 'Don'ts'. They may include: 'Don't look', 'Hide', 'Run away', 'Don't go with them', 'Say "No"', 'Don't touch', 'Tell someone'. Help the children to distinguish between those which are specific to one kind of danger only, and those which can be used in different circumstances.

Invite the children to think of some safety rules or reminders that could be used in any situation, for example:

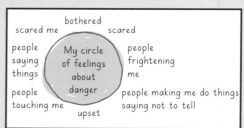

! Emphasise the importance of telling or asking someone for help and sharing one's concern. Stress that this is not the same as 'telling tales' and that most people will not laugh or disbelieve a child in trouble, and that it is important to keep on telling them your fear or problem. Practise ways of getting people to listen and finding the words which describe feelings through classroom play. **!**

Encourage the children to help you compile a 'circle of feelings' which describes how they felt when in danger. Give them the opportunity to share and reveal their concerns and fears, and to practise putting their feelings into words.

The children could role-play or mime telling someone about their fears and then share in the making of a 'circle of feelings' which describes feeling better. Emphasise again the importance of telling people how they feel. (Teachers at this stage may wish to go directly to Content box 5: Focus on people.)

Keeping myself safe

Content box 2

> *Focus on me*
> *Who am I? Where do I live?*
> *Where am I going? Where*
> *have I been? Who am I with?*
> *Who have I been with? Who is*
> *in charge? What time is it?*
> *How late is it? How do I get*
> *there? How do I ask the way*
> *or ask for help? What do*
> *'safe', 'dangerous' and 'risky'*
> *mean? What is good about*
> *being bigger and older? When*
> *is it risky? What can I do to*
> *help keep myself safe?*
> **When am I most at risk?**

Activity 1 | *Who am I? Where do I live?*

- Classroom play. Mapwork. Stories. Talking together.

- Class and group activity.

The children can practise being able to say who they are and where they live through activities centred around a topic such as the post office. You could set up a post office and sorting office in the play corner and help the children to write and sort letters and deliver cards and packages, which are addressed to themselves and people within the school.

A map of the locality with the streets, houses, shops and blocks of flats clearly labelled can give the children additional practice, not only in knowing where they live, but also in working out safe routes to get from home to other places and back again. This is a good time to ensure that they know their addresses and telephone numbers.

Many traditional stories have characters who do not know who or what they really are and where they come from, until a magical moment when all is revealed. Children will enjoy talking about these characters, for example the Ugly Duckling who did not know it was a swan, the frog who was really a prince, the servant girl who didn't know she was a princess. These stories can provide an opportunity to remind the children of the importance of knowing who they are, where they are and who is in charge.

Where are you going?

- Talking together. Giving directions.

- Class and group activity.

The ability to say where they are going and where they have been can be important safety skills for children. They can practise these skills during their everyday classroom activities and they can be reinforced when the children make outside visits.

Ask the children, before they move to a different part of the school (to the hall, cloakroom, dining room or playground), to say where they are going, how they will get there and what they think they will see or pass as they go. Afterwards they can check whether they were right. Before going on a visit away from the school, ask the children to describe the part of the route closest to the school and to practise saying who they are, the name of the school and their home or school address.

We are going to visit a farm.
We are going on a bus from the bus stop near the school.
The bus will go down a steep hill and past the station.
We have to remember:

(who we are)   (where we come from)   (where we are going)

I am
Mrs Smith.

I live at

we come from
Hillside Primary
School, Eastville

we are going to
Littlebrook Farm,
Westville

Are you sure you know who you are and where you are going?

Who is with you? Who is in charge?

- Talking together. Painting and drawing. Collecting and sorting pictures and making a display. Classroom play.

- Class and group activity.

Talk with the children about the importance of knowing who is with them and who is in charge of them or the place where they find themselves. They could talk about the different places that they go to at different times of the day. This is a good opportunity to emphasise the dangers of going into places which are closed, fenced off, etc.

Invite the children to collect or make their own pictures of children in places such as swimming pools, playgrounds, parks, river banks, beaches, shops, streets, classrooms and school visits. Display the pictures under a heading: 'Who is in charge here?'

Talk with the children about who might be in charge in each situation and how they could recognise that person. Ask the children to look at the possibility of no-one being there to take charge. Who then would be in charge? This would be a good time to help them consider the importance of being in charge of themselves and their own behaviour, and to look at the skills which they need to do this.

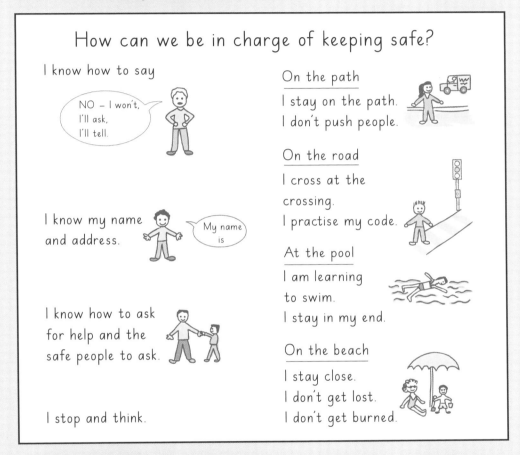

This activity provides an opportunity to identify the safe people in school, in the neighbourhood and in and around the home. You can use classroom play to share, practise and reinforce ways of approaching these people to ask for help.

Activity 4 — *Where have I been? How do I get home?*

■ Observing and describing. Drawing and painting. Sequencing pictures.

■ Class, small group and pair activity.

The skills of observing and describing sequentially where you have been can be of importance in the area of keeping safe. Young children sometimes find it difficult to describe the routes they have taken, the places they have visited and the people they have encountered. Encourage the children, particularly when they are sharing their experiences with others in the class, to try to describe places, people and routes so that others can 'see' them. Invite them to draw or paint pictures of places, events or class visits, to arrange them sequentially and to try to recall exact details.

Invite the children to recall the routes they take from their homes to school, to the shops, to places where they play and to the other homes that they visit. Ask them to pick out the danger spots along the route, for example heavy traffic, isolated or dark areas or places where people congregate. Invite the children to work in pairs or small groups and to draw themselves on some of these routes, illustrating some of the hazards (these illustrations are often very revealing). Ask the children what they would do if they needed help along the route. Where would they look? Who would they ask? Ask them to illustrate their replies.

Activity 5 — *What day is it? What time is it?*

■ Talking together. Telling the time.

■ Class and group activity.

Emphasise to the children the importance of knowing what day it is and the names of the days of the week. Encourage them to remember what happened yesterday, the day before yesterday and a week ago.

Ask the children to talk about what we do on different days of the week, at school and at home.

Encourage the children to be alert to clues about what time of day it is, whether or not it is early or late and whether or not they are early or late for some activity. You could devise activities and games in which children look for clues hidden in things they see and hear which help them estimate what time it is. For example, you could use questions and answers:

'How do you know it is time for dinner?'
'Because I am hungry.'

Encourage the children to think of more clues provided by their own feelings, for example hunger, tiredness and cold, and clues provided by their surroundings.

There are **cross-curricular links** with mathematical activities on the theme of time.

Activity 6 *What is good about being bigger and older?*

■ Talking. Writing.

■ Class and group activity.

Cross-curricular links: explore through physical education activities the children's increasing ability to reach up, to span, to jump higher and further, to balance and to control small apparatus. In language activities, help the children to talk and write about all the new things they can do, reach and control, now that they are bigger and more skilful.

Talk with the children about 'looking after yourself'. Explore questions such as:

– can you look after yourselves? all the time? some of the time?

– can you keep yourselves safe? all the time? some of the time?

– which things are risky? what might happen? how can you keep yourselves safe?

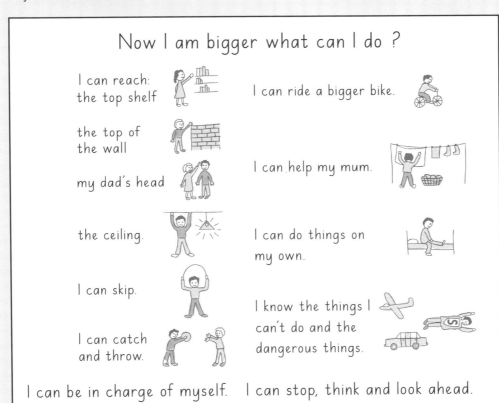

Now I am bigger what can I do ?

I can reach: the top shelf

the top of the wall

my dad's head

the ceiling.

I can skip.

I can catch and throw.

I can ride a bigger bike.

I can help my mum.

I can do things on my own.

I know the things I can't do and the dangerous things.

I can be in charge of myself.   I can stop, think and look ahead.

Activity 7 *When am I most at risk?*

■ Talking together. Describing situations and feelings. Making a display.

■ Class or group activity.

The concepts of 'taking risks' and 'being at risk' are not easy for children to grasp at this stage, but can best be explored through activities which focus on what other people do to make things risky for themselves and others. Children are often made aware of the concept of risk more effectively by observing others in risky situations, rather than by relating their own behaviour to risk taking.

Talk with the children about how they behave when they get excited, frightened, upset and angry. Ask them to think of ways in which this might affect their ability to keep themselves safe. Make a display on this theme. Remind them of the three main safety rules which they learnt earlier:

– say 'No';

– stop and think;

– ask someone for help.

Talk about the importance of keeping calm.

What do we do when we are excited?   Our feelings take charge

We jump up and down.
We shout.
We rush about.

| We forget our 'keeping safe' rules |

What do we do when we are scared?
We run away.
We don't look.
We let people bully us and make us do things.

| We forget our 'keeping safe' rules |

What do we do when we are upset?
We cry.
We don't look where we are going.
We run off.

| We forget our 'keeping safe' rules |

Keeping myself safe

Key words

rules   laws   'everywhere' rule   risks   risky   feelings   forget   target   ahead

Content box 3

3

Focus on indoors
What do I enjoy doing indoors? at home? at school? What can make play activities dangerous? What can make me safer? Is it something I can do? Who or what makes an accident happen? What are the rules indoors? Do the rules and risks depend on people and places? What am I getting better at? What would I like to be able to do? What does 'risky' mean?
When am I most at risk?

Activity 1 *What do I enjoy doing indoors?*

■ Talking and writing together. Making books. Drawing, painting and model making.

■ Class, group and individual activity.

Explore with the children the things they enjoy doing when they are indoors: at home, at other people's homes and places where they play.

Each child or group could make a 'bendy book' consisting of drawings and writing which show how they have fun and enjoy being indoors, and which says where they have fun, what they do, who is in charge of them and what day and time it is.

Make a list with the children of all the places where they play that they have included in their work. Ask them to tell you which places, and ways of playing, are dangerous. Prompt them to include stairs, cupboards, balconies, the kitchen, bathroom, swimming pools, the classroom and any local danger spots. Ask the children to look through the 'bendy books' in groups, marking the dangerous places with a red danger sign.

Encourage them to talk about what could cause an accident in these places.

Focus on:

– what the children might do;

– what others might do;

– how others might persuade them to do something which could cause an accident;

– what could happen if their feelings took charge.

Help the children to review each of these places in terms of how likely it is that accidents might happen there:

– at different times of the day;

– when they are alone;

– when they are with other people;

to help them decide when they are most at risk.

Accidents happen on the stairs

When we play about.
When it's dark.
If they are slippery.
If you're holding things.
If someone pushes you.
If you jump on them.
If someone leaves things there.
If the carpet is torn.
If you get excited.

Do's for stairs: ☺
Do – hold on
  – walk
  – look out
  – put the light on

Don'ts for stairs: ☹
Don't – jump
  – push
  – leave things there
  – play there

Is this a good place to play?   NO!

Through this kind of activity, children can learn to distinguish places which are safe to play in from those which are dangerous to play in. Invite them to make a set of 'keeping safe' rules for some of these places, for example home, school, the swimming pool. Ask them whether their rules are different for each place and help them to look for an 'everywhere' rule, one which can be applied to any place.

❗ It is important that children now begin to think beyond things, people and places as hazards, to look at situations which are *potentially* dangerous, and at the impact that their own actions have in such situations. ❗

It's safer in the classroom when:
— we stop and think
— we keep ourselves safe
— teacher is there
— we walk and don't run
— we put things away
— we listen
— we point scissors down

Can you write some more advice
for the classroom?

Accidents happen in the classroom when:
— we play about, tease, dare
— we get upset, excited, silly
— we rush about and push
— we leave things on the floor
— we come in when there is no one
  in to look after us

Can you write some more advice
for the classroom?

Talk with the children about some of the activities which are forbidden in their homes or in other people's homes which they might like to be able to do. Ask them to tell you about forbidden places which they would like to explore. Ask them what they think they would most enjoy about doing these things or going to these places? Is it the excitement? Or feeling grown-up?

Ask them to suggest the reasons people (adults?) give for not allowing them to do these things. Help them to categorise these reasons, for example:

– it belongs to someone else;

– they think I'll hurt myself;

– it's dangerous;

– it's risky;

– I couldn't do it safely;

– you have to be grown-up;

– they think I'll break it;

– I'm too small;

– they think I don't know how to do it;

– I don't know how to do it.

Talk with the children about the indoor things, places and activities which they think are *always* dangerous, for example fires and electricity. Talk about the things which could be risky, but are less risky if they have the skills to cope with them.

Encourage the children to continue to explore their list of dangerous places and to think about the different times of the day, days of the week or seasons of the year when these places may become more risky. Invite them to ask themselves the question: 'Is this a good place to play?', and help them to look for a range of answers, such as:

– no, not ever;

– only if/only when ...;

– yes, if you know the safety rules.

Explore with the children the outdoor places where they might find displayed safety rules which have been decided on by other people, for example:

– in the park (no cycling);

– by lakes, rivers and canals (no swimming, paddling);

– on electricity pylons and sub-stations;

– on escalators or in lifts;

– on railway crossings and pelican crossings;

– on building sites;

– in playgrounds.

Remind the children about rules which are good advice and rules which are laws.

Talk about the reasons for keeping the rules and the risks involved in not keeping them.

This could provide a starting point for exploring the locality of the school, for making visits and inviting safety officers to come and talk with the children.

The children could illustrate different aspects of these rules and warnings through drawing, painting or model making.

Activity 2 *What am I getting better at?*

■ Talking together. Drawing and painting.

■ Class, group and individual activity.

Talk with the children about the things that they (and you) are learning to do, and are getting better at, at home, at school and in other places, for example swimming, using scissors, doing PE, throwing and catching. Invite them to say whether these activities are risky, and what makes them so. (This can reveal a great deal about young children's perceptions of risk.)

Invite the children to illustrate this list of activities and to say what might make them risky, completing sentences as follows:

'Swimming can be risky if ...'

'Cooking can be risky when ...'

Explore with the children how they are getting better at these things. Is it just that they are older or bigger? Help them to think about generalisations like the ones below.

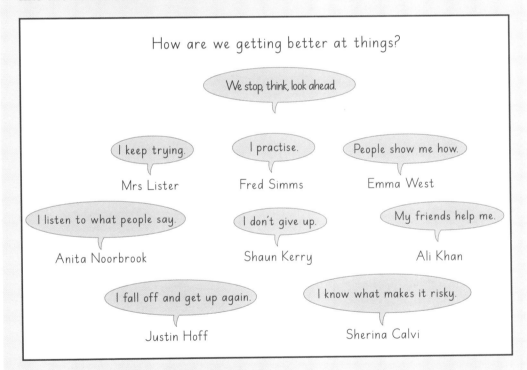

Invite the children to pick out one skill which they think they could improve and to think how they could do this and who could help them. Encourage them to set themselves a target and to ask for support from friends and family to reach that target.

Keeping myself safe

Content box 4

> **Focus on outdoors**
> *Where are the best places to play and explore? What makes these places safe, risky or dangerous? What makes them fun, exciting and interesting? What are the rules of these places? Can I remember them all? What am I getting better at? What can I learn to do so I'm safer in the street, by the water, etc? How can I learn more about being a road user?*
> **When am I most at risk?**

Activity 1 *Where are the best places to play and explore?*

- Talking together. Drawing and painting. Making a wall story or class book. Making individual books.

- Class, group and individual activity, with opportunity for family work.

Invite the children to describe, draw and paint places in the locality where they go, or have been, with the class, alone, with friends, with family, with other adults, with older children or with strangers.

What makes these places fun, exciting or interesting? What do they do there? What don't they do? When do they go? Who is in charge? Look with the children at what makes these places:

– safe;   – risky;   – dangerous.

Explore whether the risks or dangers are caused by:

– the place itself;

– the children or other people there;

– the activity itself.

Emphasise the importance of knowing and keeping the safety rules. Ask them questions such as: 'What do you do if you can't read or understand them?' The children could make a wall story or a class book illustrating these places, with the rules boldly printed.

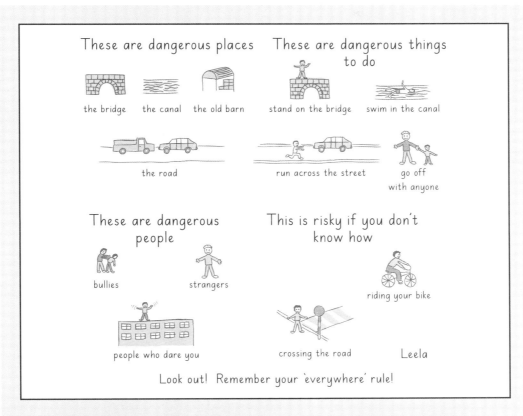

These are dangerous places

the bridge   the canal   the old barn

the road

These are dangerous things
to do

stand on the bridge   swim in the canal

run across the street   go off
with anyone

These are dangerous
people

bullies   strangers

people who dare you

This is risky if you don't
know how

riding your bike

crossing the road   Leela

Look out! Remember your 'everywhere' rule!

Invite the children to make an individual book with pictures showing themselves in some of these places keeping the rules. They could add pictures from magazines, photographs and leaflets from safety organisations.

Family work: you could suggest that the children ask their families to share in this activity, and extend the range of the books.

The children could also look at those places where there are no safety rules displayed, for example in the school playground, at zebra crossings, near the school crossing patrol, on pavements, on roads, at traffic lights, in the garden, near derelict or abandoned buildings, railways and subways. (This will provide you with opportunities to focus on specific hazards in the locality.) Remind children that not all rules and laws are written up in places for people to see, so people must learn them.

The children could work together in small groups to illustrate some of these places and to decide what the rules of these places should be. They could then compare the different sets of rules. Ask them whether or not it is possible to remember all these rules all the time.

Review the sets of rules and check how many are 'Do's' and how many are 'Don'ts'. Identify the rules which are repeated. Encourage the children to try to condense the rules into one or two which can be remembered all the time. These can be added to the children's individual books, and to the wall stories or class books.

These are my rules
for going anywhere

know   stop
the   think
dangers   ask
Paul

Activity 2 — *Learning to use the roads*

■ Talking together. Collecting and sorting pictures. Drawing. Survey work.

■ Class or group and individual activity.

Explore with the children the language of traffic. Ask them to collect pictures of traffic from magazines and sort them into categories such as lorries, vans, cars, tractors, buses.

Help the children to think about and illustrate the range of people and animals who use the roads, for example families, children, horses, drivers, delivery people, pedestrians, traffic wardens, police, crossing patrol, building workers.

Help them to think about and illustrate the different areas and places where traffic is found, for example roads, streets, pavements, footpaths, driveways, entrances, exits, car parks, bus stops, zebra crossings, pelican crossings, traffic lights, traffic islands, subways.

The children could carry out a simple survey of the traffic and people passing the school gate at different times of the day. Help them to decide when it is most dangerous and what are the important rules to follow at these times. You can give them clues: 'What makes being in traffic risky?' 'What makes it safer?'

Invite the children to look at the skills for dealing with traffic which they can practise, for example stopping, moving, listening and looking. Talk about how they can recognise danger:

– as they go out of the school gate;

– on the pavement;

– when getting ready to cross the road;

– when crossing the road;

– when alone;

– with friends;

– with adults;

– when going out to play.

A similar approach could be used in order to focus on other areas of risk in the locality, for example railway lines, bridges and canals.

- Drawing and writing. Talking together.

- Class or group and individual activity.

You could adapt the 'Draw and write' technique (see Introduction and Appendix 1) to investigate what the children think they are getting better at doing outdoors and what they now think they need to keep safe from.

Without any prior discussion or sharing of ideas, ask the children to draw themselves outdoors, doing some of the things they are becoming better at. Ask them to label their pictures, starting with these words: 'I am getting better at ...'.

There is a **cross-curricular link** with mathematical representation: you could either analyse their replies and present your analysis to them, or you could help them to present the investigation results themselves. Use bar charts or any other methods of mathematical representation you think appropriate.

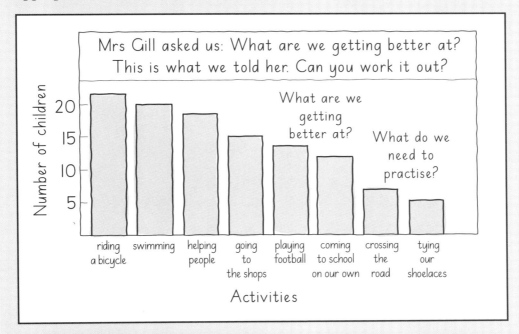

The children could then identify those skills which they as individuals think they most need to improve or extend.

They could make contracts with themselves and pinpoint ways in which they might best succeed, for example:

- by practising;

- asking for help;

- observing others;

- learning the rules;

- remembering the risks;

- identifying people at home, in school and in the local community who could help them fulfil their contracts.

Keeping myself safe

Key words

recognise   team   safe   responsible   threaten   trust   tell   rules   vote
'everywhere' rule

Content box 5

> **5**
>
> *Focus on people*
> *Who will help me to keep safe? How do I recognise people whose job it is to keep me safe? What are they trying to teach us to do, or not to do? How can I help them? How do I know who to ask for help? Who are the people who threaten my safety? How do I recognise them? How can I keep myself safe?*
> ***When am I most at risk?***

Activity 1 *Who will help to keep me safe?*

■ Talking together. Sharing stories and television programmes. Collecting and sorting pictures. Drawing and painting. Making a collage. Visits. Role-play.

■ Class or group and individual activity.

Cross-curricular links: this activity can form an important strand in a more general topic such as: 'People who help us'.

Explore with the children what they would do if they lost something or became lost themselves. Use their experiences, a story or a television programme as a starting point. This could be an opportunity to reinforce the work on the theme: 'Who am I? Where do I live?' from Content box 2.

Who helps to keep us safe?

The keeping safe team:

mums
dads
family
friends

US
we help to
keep ourselves
safe

police officers
fire brigade
crossing patrol
teachers

It might also be prudent to remind children about the dangers of agreeing to anyone's requests for help in searching for lost things or pets.

Invite the children to help you to collect pictures from magazines, photographs and posters. Combine these with their own drawings and paintings of people who help to keep them safe, and arrange them in a collage. Encourage them to include pictures of family, friends, teachers and members of the community. Ask each child to add a picture of herself or himself as a very important part of this team.

Explore with the children the roles of some of these helpers.

– Do they wear uniforms? Can they describe them?

– How do we recognise helpers if they do not have uniforms?

– What kind of job is it? Is it risky? What makes it risky?

– What do they have to do so it's not so risky?

– What do they do every day?

– What do they do in emergencies?

– What do they do to stop people getting hurt?

– What do they try to teach us?

– What are their messages to grown-ups and children?

You could use visits, visitors, recall, observation, role-play and creative activities to help the children find the answers to these questions. You could display safety messages from different helpers as reminders and reinforcement.

Ask the children to reflect on what they can do to help these people and to take on their share of the job. Help them to consider:

– learning the messages and keeping the rules;

– being aware of what makes the helpers' jobs difficult;

– practising getting better at doing things;

– being aware of the risks;

– setting a good example and passing on the messages.

Remind the class that this is part of being a good citizen.

Ask the children if it is possible to take all these people with them wherever they go. Is it possible to remember all their messages? What can they do if it isn't possible? Would it be helpful to reduce all the messages to one or two important ones which could help them in any situation? Write up all their suggestions and vote on the best 'everywhere' rule.

Activity 2 — *Who are the people who threaten my safety?*

■ Drawing and writing. Talking together. Role-play.

■ Class or group and individual activity.

It is important to tap the children's perceptions of people who they see as threatening, and to explore with them how they think these people can, or do, harm them, and how they can be recognised. Many children have a stereotyped picture of people with whom they could be at risk, and this is based almost completely on appearance.

It would be valuable to adapt and use the 'Draw and write' technique at this point (see Introduction and Appendix 1 for more information). Invite the children, without discussion, to draw themselves keeping safe from dangerous people, and to label or describe the person, the danger and their method of keeping safe.

Children may name specific people in their replies or respond in more general terms, for example strangers or people who tease, dare, threaten, vandalise, bully, sniff glue, touch, scare and abuse. You will undoubtedly uncover aspects of the children's perceptions, fears or misunderstandings which are not covered here, but which need to be followed up.

Explore this question with the children: 'How can we tell this is a dangerous person?' Help them to focus less on appearance and more on the kinds of things these people might say or do. Challenge stereotypical views of strangers and others.

Explore with the children some of the best strategies for dealing with these situations, for example:

- stay with people you know, like and trust;

- don't join other groups or follow older children;

- get help from people you can trust;

- tell other people about what happened, where it happened and how you felt;

- say 'No, don't', 'I'll ask someone', etc.

Provide opportunities for the children to practise these strategies using role-play and working out in the community.

Cross-curricular link: use stories and poems to illustrate how to deal with threatening people. Contact your children's librarian for help or compile your own list of relevant material.

Reflection and action

Look back with the children at the five aspects of keeping safe that they have been working with:
- keeping their feelings safe;
- keeping themselves safe;
- keeping safe indoors;
- keeping safe outdoors;
- being safe with people.

- Ask them to recall the people 'out there' in their community whose job it is to keep people and places safe, healthy and happy. Talk about other 'good citizens' – ordinary people who they know they can trust to help when needed.
- Remind them of their rule: 'Stop! Think! Look ahead!', and how keeping that rule makes people's jobs much easier.
- Look back at the difference between rules of different places and laws of the country.
- Ask them to practise their own classroom and school rules and their 'everywhere' rule, and to share their worries with a trusted grown-up. Remind them that there are people in school to help.

Key theme 3: Me and my relationships

The six content boxes on page 173 each have a distinctive focus and act as starting points for the classroom activities. The questions in each content box stimulate discussion and help you to build on previous skills and knowledge and to identify where the children are in their understanding.

It is important that you select and extend the classroom activities according to: your PSHE or PSD and Citizenship programmes; your school's mission statement regarding the values central to your school; your school's behaviour policy; your programme for Assembly and/or corporate acts of Worship; your Healthy School initiatives; your school's sex education policy and programme.

Focus of teaching
Widening understanding of self and others, their feelings (including adults); recognising and valuing others' possessions, preferences; differentiating between hurt feelings/physical hurts, understanding physical differences between girls and boys as they grow up; understanding parenting skills and the needs of babies and young children; understanding the importance of loving human relationships; tackling gender stereotyping; recognising that quarrels, break up of friendships and family relationships, separation and loss, do occur, and the need for coping skills; recognising the impact of bullying on people's happiness and self-esteem; widening understanding of their growing responsibilities.

Key skills and competencies
Empathy; describing and categorising feelings, views and attitudes; describing and contrasting people, places, situations; reflecting on outcomes; recognising pressure; refusal skills; coping skills; widening the language of feelings using adjectives and adjectival phrases; differentiating skills; working within rule-based situations; story telling; generalising from many rules to one rule.

Citizenship opportunities
Opportunities to: work with people who manage the environment; and understand their roles, rules, by-laws and laws of the country. Tackle specific issues that arise in your school and community; work with children's after-school clubs and groups; hold class and group discussions relating to the reality of their environment.

Links with children's literature
Stories where characters: learn they are emotionally stronger than they thought; take risks and learn from these situations; put their feelings about their relationships, home and school into words. Stories about loving relationships, loss or separation being shared and coped with.

Me and my relationships

1

Focus on special people

Who are my special people? What do we do together? How do I know when people are special to me? How do we tell each other we are special? How do my special people and I make each other happy? How do they make me feel clever, excited, safe or hurt? When is it OK to say 'No'? Who can I tell if saying 'No' is difficult? When is it OK to pretend and when is it dangerous? Do grown-ups pretend sometimes?

2

Focus on friends and friendship

What is a friend? Who are my best friends or my oldest friends? When have friends helped me? What good bargains have we made with our friends? What are bad bargains? How do we deal with bullies? How do I make friends? How can I get to know what people are really like? How do I feel when things get broken? How do I feel when friendships are broken? How can people stay friends? Are pretend people, or people from television programmes or stories, friends? What can I do about real people who might pretend?

3

Focus on feelings

When have I felt too excited to sleep or eat? Why did I feel this way? When did I feel this way? When have I felt bullied, upset, angry or scared? How did I cope? How do people look when they are angry? What happens when people around me quarrel? Do they mean what they say? How do I feel after I quarrel with someone? How do I feel when I am left out? How do I feel when my special people go away or die? How can I tell people how I feel?

4

Focus on memories

What are my special belongings? Who is allowed to touch them? Is my body one of these special belongings? Who is allowed to touch it? What is the difference between hurting my knee and hurting my feelings? What makes these hurts better? How can I help people feel better? What can I remember about growing up? What were the funniest, saddest or noisiest times? Who shares my memories?

5

Focus on special places

What makes some places special to me? What makes our classroom special? How do we keep it looking and feeling good? What spoils it? How do we feel if places are dirty or broken up? Where do I feel happy and safe? Which are the places I wouldn't go to? Which places are special to other people or to our pets? What can we do to keep their places happy for them?

6

On a day like today

What are the things I do on a day like today on my own? with help? What do I think I would be doing on a day like today if I were a mum or a dad with my own family? What if I were a mum growing a new baby inside me? How are babies cared for before they are ready to be born, and afterwards when they are new? Why do we grow up so slowly? What do we need to learn so we can be good mums and dads?

Key messages
for me and my relationships

Learn:

- the names of your special people, both the names you know them by and the names they use for each other;
- how to make people feel better;
- about making friends and sharing things with your friends;
- that other people may live lives which are different from yours;
- that when we move house we have to build up another network of friends which can be hard;
- that girl babies are born, grow up into women and when they are ready can have a family with babies of their own;
- that boy babies are born, grow up into men and when they are ready can have a family with babies of their own;
- that you need a man and a woman to make a new baby;
- that babies need love and care in their families for a long time and it can be very hard work.

Understand:

- that as you make more friends it is as if a network of people grows around you;
- that the people in your network are special to one another in different ways and sometimes you may feel left out;
- that you and the people in your network can make each other happy, sad or angry, but still care about each other;
- that people pretend or hide their feelings sometimes so they don't worry you;
- that pretending or keeping secrets can be frightening and dangerous and you must tell someone you trust – it is not the same as 'telling tales';
- that friendships can be broken but that they can also be mended again;
- that sometimes your family will not like your friends, and although this is worrying, it is best to talk about it;
- that when people in your network go away or die it is not your fault, it may be for reasons you don't understand;
- that your body is your very own. Take care of it and keep it healthy and safe.

Practise:

- telling a safe person if you are frightened or worried;
- saying 'No' if someone is trying to hurt or frighten you;
- helping people who don't have friends;
- respecting other people's things and places.

Share these key messages with parents, families and people in the community so that they can support and reinforce them.

Me and my relationships

Content box 1

1

Focus on special people
Who are my special people?
What do we do together? How
do I know when people are
special to me? How do we tell
each other we are special?
How do my special people and
I make each other happy?
How do they make me feel
clever, excited, safe or hurt?
When is it OK to say 'No'?
Who can I tell if saying 'No' is
difficult? When is it OK to
pretend and when is it
dangerous? Do grown-ups
pretend sometimes?

Activity 1 *Who are my special people?*

- Links with literature. Talking together. Drawing and painting. Making a collage or chart. Classroom play.

- Class or group and individual activity.

The children could take as their starting point the central character from a story which you have read to them. With the children's help draw the character's network of special people.

Talk with the children about how the characters in the story related to one another? Which people knew each other? Who knew about each other but never met? Who didn't know about the others? Explore how the central character might have felt if people in the network had not liked each other.

Grandpa's adventure

Grandpa knew them all.
Grandma didn't know Barny or Tenko.
Grandma knew Jo, Jenny and the paper boy.
Tenko didn't know anyone but Grandpa.
Grandma wouldn't like Barny and Tenko.
Jo and Jenny would like Barny if they met him.
Grandpa didn't tell Grandma about
Tenko or Barny.
She'd have gone mad!   Freddie

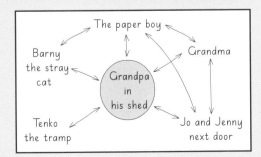

Help the children to understand that everyone lives within a network of people and that tensions between these people are common. Some children may be able to use the network of the characters in the story as a model for constructing and exploring their own networks.

Invite the children to draw pictures of their special people and the other people in their network, or to bring to school photographs of them, and make them into a collage or network chart. They could include in this network their immediate and extended families, people they see infrequently and friends in and out of school. It is important to behave sensitively to children who have few special people, no family or families which are going through separation.

Explore with the children why these people are special. For example: 'We like each other', 'We belong together', 'We play together', 'We look after each other', 'We have special names for each other', 'We have special ways of saying hello and goodbye'. The idea of unique relationships existing between and among people is not easy to grasp but the children's responses will indicate their level of awareness. Encourage them to illustrate their responses in drawing, painting and classroom play.

Talk with the children about how they are special: the unique way each of them looks and sounds, and their unique role in their own special network. Help them to write down how they are special. Ask each of the children to draw a picture of herself or himself, with a speech bubble saying, 'This is me. I'm special.'

Talk about the ways in which people tell the children they are special without using the word 'special' or without using words.

Ask the children to think of ways in which they tell their special people how special they are, in words or actions. For example: 'I say, "I love you"'; 'I say, "You make the best chips in the world"'; 'I say, "I missed you"'; 'I say, "I like it best when you are here"'; 'I play with the baby to help'. Remind the children that it is important to tell people that they are valued, missed and loved.

Activity 2 *How do my special people and I make each other happy?*

■ Drawing and writing. Making books. Analysing. Categorising. Talking together.

■ Class or group and individual activity.

Ask the children (without any prior discussion) to draw themselves making their special people happy. Ask them to write at the side of each of their pictures what it is they are doing, or if they cannot write to whisper to you so you can write for them.

The children's perceptions of their roles in these relationships can be very revealing. A simple method of discovering this is by using the 'Draw and write' technique (see Introduction and Appendix 1). The children could help you to analyse and present the results pictorially. Together look at the similarities and differences in their views.

This activity could be repeated by asking the children to draw themselves making their special people worried, angry, sad or proud of them. The children could make individual illustrated books showing how their behaviour has an impact on their special people, and share them with other children to look for similarities and differences.

Invite the children to repeat the previous activity, this time looking at what their special people do to make them happy. Encourage them to share in analysing their responses. How many children are made happy by gifts? How many are aware that love, care and family life make them happy?

Repeat the activity asking them to draw their special people making them feel safe, not so safe, worried, proud, clever, excited, shy or silly.

This exploration of the children's perceptions of what makes them feel unsafe, hurt or unsure could provide a springboard for the introduction of more specific material related to child abuse and 'keeping safe' skills.

Saying 'No', 'Stop', 'Don't do that to me' is difficult for young children, and is even more difficult when it has to be said to their special people. They will need help and practice in the skills of handling these situations, finding someone to tell, making someone listen and having the language with which to explain.

Activity 3 *When is it OK to pretend?*

■ Talking together. Creative play. Drawing and writing.

■ Class or group and individual activity, with opportunity for family work.

Some children may feel it is necessary for them to pretend not to be upset by some of the things their special people say, do or ask them to do. It is important that children are helped to differentiate between the pretending which is good or fun, and pretending which is dangerous or potentially dangerous.

Invite the children to make small-scale people using paper, card, scrap materials, wooden spoons, etc. They could also bring their own puppets or action figures to school. Encourage them to use these to role-play imaginary and real stories of all kinds, with or without audience participation.

Talk with the children about this kind of pretending, and about the fun of being the hero or the 'baddy', and being brave, clever and different. Ask them to remember times when they might dress up as someone else, for example when they take part in a class or school play.

Encourage the children to think about other kinds of pretending, for example:

– pretending something doesn't hurt, such as a cut knee or an injection;

– pretending someone hasn't hurt your feelings, frightened you or made you worried;

We are pretending

I am pretending
I am the caretaker.
That's fun.

Our baby pulls my hair.
He loves it –
I am pretending
I do. It's OK for him
– not me.

I am pretending I like
Sullah's cake. I don't
like to upset her.
That's OK.

We are dressing up.
That's fun
pretending.

I am pretending my
knee doesn't hurt.
I am being brave.
That's good.

I am pretending
I like being tickled.
It's not good. I am
going to say
NO DON'T
and tell my mum.

I am pretending I
like being called
names, but I don't.
That's bullying
and it's not fun.

- pretending you like being hugged, tickled, touched, picked up or teased;

- pretending you don't mind being called pet names or unkind names;

- pretending which is really bullying.

There are opportunities here to work on aspects of gender, exploring ideas such as: 'only girls cry', 'boys have to be brave', 'these are boys' clothes ... games', etc.

Invite the children to talk, illustrate and write about different kinds of pretending and to decide whether the pretence was good or whether it could be dangerous, and what they would do if they felt threatened, bullied or worried.

Grown-ups pretend sometimes

Mrs McCormick pretends she's gone deaf because we shout. That's funny.

My mum pretends she's forgotten to buy our tea. I know she hasn't.

My dad pretends he's a hungry bear and he's going to eat us up. I like it when he pretends like that.

Auntie Lou pretends she doesn't know me because I've grown big. She does really.

The police officer told us there was a man pretending he had lost his dog to get us to go with him. We wouldn't go.

This could be an opportunity to reinforce 'keeping safe' skills, looking in particular at situations where people not known to them may pretend they need the children's help, or have messages for them, while having ulterior motives.

Family work: the success of the work on pretending requires that, wherever possible, it is shared with and reinforced by the children's family network and the wider community. The children will need constant reassurance, in and out of school, that saying 'No', 'Stop', 'That's not true' and 'I'll ask' is the way to deal with pretending which makes them feel uneasy or unsafe, and that they will not get into trouble for behaving in this way. They will need reassurance too that there is always someone in the school who will listen to their concerns.

Me and my relationships

Key words

network   feelings   broken   mend   real   pretend   quarrel   look ahead   bullies

Content box 2

2

Focus on friends and friendship
What is a friend? Who are my best friends or my oldest friends? When have friends helped me? What good bargains have we made with our friends? What are bad bargains? How do we deal with bullies? How do I make friends? How can I get to know what people are really like? How do I feel when things get broken? How do I feel when friendships are broken? How can people stay friends? Are pretend people, or people from television programmes or stories, friends? What can I do about real people who might pretend?

Activity 1   *What is a friend?*

- Talking together. Drawing and painting. Making a collage. Classroom play, movement and drama. Making a display. Writing.

- Class or group and individual activity.

Talk with the children about the friends they have made in school, out of school or in other places. Ask them to make a picture or collage of their network of friends. They can start by putting their self-portrait in the centre and grouping around it photographs or drawings of their school friends, old friends, best friends, new friends, etc.

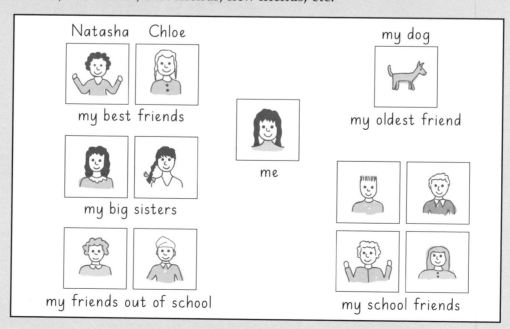

Invite the children to share their work with others. Some children may have included imaginary friends, pets, older brothers and sisters and adults, and this can be the starting point for discussion of what friends are or can be.

It is important to be sensitive to the feelings of children who are new to the class, who do not make friends easily or are shunned for some reason.

Invite the children to think about all the things friends do with and for each other. Make a note of their suggestions and explore them further using classroom play, painting, movement and drama.

Are there rules for keeping friends? Collect up their suggested rules. The children could make a display of books, stories, poems and pictures about friends and friendship and add to it their own pictures and writing.

Talk with the children about the things good friends do for them. Invite them to recall times when a good friend, or someone in the family network, helped them. How did it feel to have a good friend? Ask the children to recall times when *they* acted as a good friend to someone else. How did it feel to be the good friend? Look for words to help children express the feelings and friendship.

Activity 2 *Good bargains and bad bargains*

■ Classroom play. Talking together. Links with literature.

■ Class and group activity.

Use classroom play to enact 'If you do this ... then I'll do that ...' situations.

– 'If you are quick to tidy up, then we can have a story.' (Teacher and class.)

– 'If you help with the baby, I'll get your tea ready.' (Adult and child.)

– 'If you help me with this writing, I'll help you to glue your model.' (Children.)

Ask the children to invent more examples. Talk with them about keeping bargains such as these. Who feels good when they work? What are the results?

We made some good bargains this week

Mrs Wilson said if we cleaned out the hamsters we could play with them.

I helped Sammy with some work and she helped me make my puppet.

My dad made a bargain with me. I helped clean the car and he took me fishing.

I made a bargain with Joe and Sam. I wouldn't get in their way and they would stop teasing me.

These are good bargains. We got lots done.

Talk with the children about 'bad bargains', which are one-sided or threatening, and which people could use to bully children, lead them into danger or persuade them not to tell anyone. There are many examples of these in children's literature which you could use as starting points for a discussion with the children. They could make a collection of examples of 'bad bargains' in stories and from their own experience.

This would be a good opportunity to remind the children of the school's policy on bullying and the importance of telling an adult what is happening.

Activity 3 *Making friends and breaking friends*

■ Classroom play. Talking together. Collecting and categorising. Making a 'circle of feelings'. Drawing and writing.

■ Class or group and individual activity.

Set the scene with a story outline, for example a new child has joined the class and is shy and knows no one. Using body language and role-play explore with the children how the new child might look, speak, move and feel when he or she is without friends but wants to make friends.

Tammy is new to the class. She feels shy. She wants to make friends.
She is thinking ○ ○
(Nobody is going to want to be my friend.)

She looks like this. You can see she is shy.

What could we do to help?

We could say ⟨ Hello! Can I be your friend? Do you want to play? ⟩

We could share things — show her the way.

The midday helpers could look after her.

We could say ⟨ You'll like our class — it's the greatest. ⟩

Mrs Joseph could tell her we're friendly.

Jimmy looks very big and rough. I was scared of him at first.

Inside he's a bit shy and very kind. He's my friend.

Leslie can't talk very well. I couldn't tell what she said at first.

Inside she's so funny and makes me laugh. She plays good games. She's my friend.   Sharon

Ask the children to explain how they decide to be friends with someone. What helps them to decide? Is the way the person looks important? How would they get to know what the person is like inside?

Invite the children to make a collection of broken things which they have found in the classroom, the neighbourhood and at home. Ask the children to group the items,

all my fault

clumsy

cross with myself

fed up

Our feelings about breaking things and broken things

mad

cross with who did it

sad

worried

in trouble

heart broken

using categories such as: 'Someone broke these', 'You can mend these', 'You can't mend these'.

Ask the children how they feel when they break things or when they see broken things. Make a note of the language they use and write it down in the form of a 'circle of feelings'. Invite the children to draw and write about their own experience of breaking things or finding broken things.

We think you can mend these things with:

glue   nails   a new bit   string   help

Mrs Khanna says you can mend things with love.

Ask the children what they do with the things which cannot be mended, for example do they:

- keep the bits;
- throw them away;
- forget about it;
- keep remembering it;

- get a new one;
- cry;
- tell someone.

How do they feel?

Talk with the children (or begin by using a story or classroom play) about how it feels when a special friend goes away, moves house or changes schools. How does it feel to be the one left behind? How can they keep in touch and remember the friend and the friendship?

Look back with the children at their work on broken things. What else, besides moving house, can break friendships? Help them to think about quarrels, misunderstandings and the attraction of new friendships. How does it feel when friendships get broken? Can these be forgotten or repaired with glue and nails? Explore with the children the ways in which they can stay friends with people, for example:

- not being bossy;
- not being unkind;
- saying 'Sorry' first;

- helping each other;
- sharing and taking turns.

Activity 4 *Imaginary friends*

- Talking together, using literature and television programmes. Writing and drawing.

- Class or group and individual activity.

Stories, poems, television programmes, comics and cartoons often feature imaginary friends who are sometimes visible, and sometimes invisible. These friends may play important roles, providing company, good advice, a conscience and specific skills. Invite the children to make a list or collection of stories which feature this kind of 'pretend friend'.

Explore some of the stories to discover why the character needed a pretend friend and what their pretend friend did. Ask the children whether they have had, or still have, pretend friends.

We have been playing pretend friends

Harry had a pretend dog in the story. He couldn't have a real one in the flats.

Micky had a pretend friend. He was scared of the dark.

Naim had a pretend friend, so she always got two sweets.

Louella in the film had a pretend sister. She really had 6 brothers.

Grizelda had a pretend friend. It made all the mess.

Someone wanted Smithy to be his secret friend, but Smithy said NO. It was on the video we saw. We all said NO.

Traditional stories and fables can provide a useful starting point for looking at the more threatening aspects of pretence, for example 'bad' characters use a disguise (*Little Red Riding Hood*). Invite the children to look beneath these characters' disguises and their seemingly innocuous actions, and think about their real motives.

A pretend friend – BEWARE!

Encourage the children to illustrate some of these situations. Use speech bubbles to help them describe what is being said and thought bubbles to capture the real intentions of the bad characters.

There are opportunities here to talk with the children about ways of avoiding potentially dangerous situations and places, and to practise 'keeping safe' skills.

Me and my relationships

Key words

feelings   behave   quarrel   faces   left out   hurtful   upset   tell

Content box 3

3

Focus on feelings
When have I felt too excited to sleep or eat? Why did I feel this way? When did I feel this way? When have I felt bullied, upset, angry or scared? How did I cope? How do people look when they are angry? What happens when people around me quarrel? Do they mean what they say? How do I feel after I quarrel with someone? How do I feel when I am left out? How do I feel when my special people go away or die? How can I tell people how I feel?

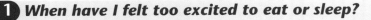

Activity 1 **When have I felt too excited to eat or sleep?**

■ Talking together. Making a 'circle of feelings'. Making a collage. Writing.

■ Class or group activity.

Talk with the children about the times when they have felt too excited to sleep or eat. How did it feel? When and why did they feel this way? Was it before or after some special time? What happened in the end? Make a note of the language they use and write it down as a 'circle of feelings'.

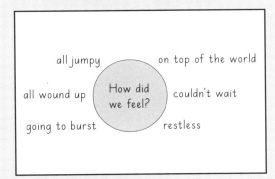

Invite the children to make a collage of pictures (either their own or pictures cut from magazines) showing people who are highly excited, and to add to it their own descriptive words and phrases.

Explore the children's memories of other times when they had strong feelings. Can they remember the times when they felt bullied, teased, upset or scared? Was it something they themselves did? Or something someone else did? Or something they were afraid might happen? What did they do to help themselves feel better? Did they tell someone? What did they say to make the person listen?

Activity 2 — What happens when people quarrel?

- Talking together. Links with literature.

- Class or group activity.

Describe a situation in which two children are fighting – it could be in the playground, the classroom or at home. They look as though they are hurting each other, but when they are stopped by adults they say, 'We were only playing'. Invite the children to think about the adult. What made the adult think it was a quarrel? Was it the noise? Or the physical violence? Ask the children to talk about times when they have seen people who look as though they are quarrelling. Have the children ever been mistaken?

When I'm in a quarrel:

I shout and I get a red face — Thomas

I cry and I ran away one time — Ranjit

I shout and hit people — Fiona

After the quarrel I feel:

sorry   sad   fed up

stupid   silly   still angry

like making friends again

Talk with the children about how it feels to be in a quarrel with friends or grown-ups. What do they do? What do they want to do? How do they feel afterwards? Make a note of the children's vocabulary and encourage them to broaden it. Some children may use the words 'silly' or 'stupid' frequently at this age to express a range of meanings.

This is an opportunity for children to talk about how they feel when quarrels happen around them, particularly in their networks of family and friends. It is important for the children to understand that quarrels do and will happen around them, and that they are rarely the cause.

There are many picture books and stories which you can use so the children can share the feelings other children have about quarrels and quarrelling. Ask them to look at how the characters in stories react and how they deal with the situation. What might they themselves have done?

Activity 3 — How do I feel when I am left behind or left out?

- Talking together. Links with literature. Painting, drawing and collecting pictures. Classroom play.

- Class or group activity.

Ask the children to look for poems, stories or news items which are about things or people being left behind.

Encourage the children to contribute their own recollections, their paintings or drawings on this subject or pictures cut from magazines. Invite the children to put themselves in the place of a story character who has been left behind, and explore the situation through classroom play. How did the character feel? Did the character think he/she was left behind for ever? Encourage the children to think about why people and things get left behind. Help them to ask questions such as: 'Was it because the person ran off?' 'Was it because the person was a girl?'

Left behind

Tolly was left behind in the story. He felt sad. No one wanted him.
Patsy

I got left behind because it was just for grown ups. I was mad.
Sylvester

I got left behind because I'm a girl. The boys went. It's not fair.
Lucy

The boy got left behind the piper because he had a gammy leg.
David

This activity could provide a springboard for some children to talk through some of their own hurtful experiences of being left behind or left out. It might also provide an opening for some children to talk through their feelings about people who were special to them, but who went away and failed to return, or who died. There is strong evidence that young children need to ask questions and be given answers about separation (temporary or permanent) and about loss and death. Where there is separation, or the break up of a family or death, young children are often excluded as adults are fearful of distressing them, or they are told to keep out of the way in order not to add to the adults' distress. Many children recall this later as a sign that they were in some way responsible.

Sam's dog died. He was very old.

Sam cried.  He loved his dog.

He told us all the funny tricks his dog did.

We were sad for Sam.

Ellie's big sister went away.

Ellie cried. She loved her big sister.

They are going to write lots of letters.

We are going to help Ellie with her letters.

Me and my relationships

Key words

share   value   respect   spoil   hurt   feelings   comfort   memories

Content box 4

4

Focus on memories
What are my special belongings? Who is allowed to touch them? Is my body one of these special belongings? Who is allowed to touch it? What is the difference between hurting my knee and hurting my feelings? What makes these hurts better? How can I help people feel better? What can I remember about growing up? What were the funniest, saddest or noisiest times? Who shares my memories?

Activity 1   *My special belongings*

■ Categorising. Talking together. Writing and drawing.

■ Class or group and individual activity, with opportunity for family work.

Ask the children to look in the box or drawer where they keep the things they use in school and to sort out what is there, grouping them into categories such as:

– these belong to the class;

– these belong to someone else;

– these are the things I share;

– these are the things which belong to me and are special to me.

These are my special things

My new hat my gran sent me.

I am Raphina

My last lot of birthday cards.

My old teddy – I take it to bed.

My body – I don't like people pushing me about.

My cat – it loves me.

The red plate – I lend it to my brother sometimes.

My crayons – they do good pictures. I don't like lending them.

Talk with the children about the special belongings which they keep at home and at school.

Talk with the children about where they keep these special things, when they use them and whether they like to share them with other people. Children do not find it easy to pin down what makes their things special but are very aware of their feelings of personal possession. Invite the children to make and illustrate their own charts, and to share them with others so that they can become more sensitive to other people's feelings.

Family work: the children could take home their charts, explain them to their families and ask them to add their comments and illustrations.

Take this activity one step further by asking the children to make charts showing the special belongings of members of their family network or their network of friends.

Encourage the children to explore ways in which they can show other people that they respect their belongings, for example by not touching them, by asking the owner first and by taking care of them.

This activity could provide an opportunity to introduce or reinforce the children's understanding that their bodies (and the space immediately around them) are very special and belong to them alone, and that they can (and must) seek help if they are uneasy or frightened about the way others touch them.

Activity 2 | ***What is the difference between hurting my knee and hurting my feelings?***

- Talking together. Role-play.

- Class or group activity.

Recall with the children the work they did on broken things and broken friendships (Content box 2, pages 180–184) and how these might or might not be mended. Explore with the children how they and other people feel if one of their special belongings is spoiled, broken or used by someone else. How hurt would they feel? Ask them to think about the difference between being hurt by falling down, and having their feelings hurt.

Hurt knees and hurt feelings

I have fallen over
and hurt my knee.
I am bleeding and crying.
I want a plaster and a
wash to make me better
and a cuddle.
My body is hurt.

Sherina

My feelings are hurt.
There is no blood or dirt.
I am crying. A plaster
isn't any good.
I want someone to
make me better.

Timmy

Discuss what we can do when we feel hurt, for example find someone to tell or do something else with a friend. Who could they tell? What would they say? Help the children to role-play some situations in which they can be the comforter, the person who is hurt or the person saying 'I'm sorry'.

This is an opportunity to include some early discussion on First Aid.

Talk with the children about how they might help a friend whose feelings had been hurt. What could they say or do?

Activity 3 *What can I remember?*

■ Talking together. Recall. Organising memories. Presenting information.

■ Class or group and individual activity, with opportunity for family work.

Ask the children to talk about the times they remember most. What can they remember about being a baby, a toddler, starting school? Ask them to bring in school photographs of themselves, or they could draw pictures to help them remember. What are the happiest, funniest, noisiest or saddest times they remember? When were they most surprised, angry, disappointed or jealous?

Help them to make individual books, or a class book or wall chart to display their memories and help them to share their personal experiences. **Family work:** invite the children's family network to contribute. What do they most remember about the child, the birth, the worrying and happy times, the funny and sad times? The sharing of memories is an important aspect of relationships and self-esteem, and can be reinforced through family involvement.

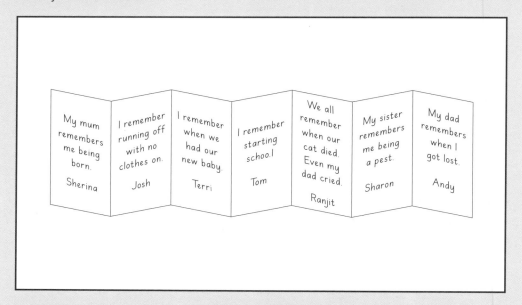

Invite the children to return to their work on networks (Content boxes 1 and 2, pages 175–179, 180–184) and pick out the people who have known them for a long time, the people with whom they share school memories, and the people who have joined their networks recently.

Me and my relationships

Key words

special   value   spoil   vandals   noise   peaceful   rules   laws   complain

Content box 5

5

Focus on special places
What makes some places special to me? What makes our classroom special? How do we keep it looking and feeling good? What spoils it? How do we feel if places are dirty or broken up? Where do I feel happy and safe? Which are the places I wouldn't go to? Which places are special to other people or to our pets? What can we do to keep their places happy for them?

Activity 1 *What makes some places special to me?*

- Talking together. Making a chart. Writing, drawing, painting and model-making.

- Class and group activity.

Cross-curricular links: this work links with topic work which explores the immediate locality, and with visits to places of interest.

Talk with the children about the places in and around the school which are special to them and to people they know. Help them to make an illustrated chart which can be added to over time.

Remind the children of the rules of different places and why we have and need rules and laws.

Encourage the children to look at their classroom. If they were showing visitors around what would they want to show them? How would the visitors know the room was special? What would the visitors see or not see? Who keeps the classroom happy, looking good and special? What do they do? Who brings things to school? What spoils it? Who spoils it? What can we do about it? Extend the work to look in the same way at the school, the playground and other places which the children think are special. How do they feel when these places are happy and well cared for? How do they feel when these places are dirty, broken up or spoiled?

Our special places

The play park is special, but it gets spoiled.

We had a special day out at the wildlife park.

The big library is special to us. We went and had a story.

Our garden is special to us.

This is our school – it is very special to us.

Our classroom is special to our class.

Class 2

Where we live is special.

The Day Centre is special to lots of people. We went to sing for them.

The clinic is special for babies.

They all have different rules.

There are opportunities here to look with the children at places in the locality which people are making special efforts to improve, or where there are particular problems relating to litter or vandalism. How can they help these people and make their jobs easier to do? This would be a good opportunity to learn about the local departments and their different responsibilities in keeping places safe and healthy.

Ask the children to describe the places which are special to them within the school environment, for example the places where they and their friends like to talk, play, share things or hide from others.

Ask the children to work in groups and use writing, drawing, painting and model-making to describe and explore these special places. Can they say which places are small and quiet and can be used as a retreat? Which places are used for imaginative play and physical activity? Are any of these places dangerous or secret? How do they take care of these special places? How do they feel if people spoil them?

Our special place

This is our special place in the corner of the playground. We pretend it's all kinds of things like a space ship or a cave.

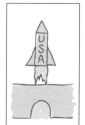

We don't let anyone throw things on the ground or mess it up. We call it our place.

Group 1   Alice   Ben   Henry   Yula

Activity 2 *Places I wouldn't go to. Other people's special places.*

- Links with literature. Talking together. Making a collage. Drawing and writing. Making a display.

- Class or group activity.

Using children's literature which deals with imaginary fantasy worlds could be a starting point for exploring places which the children might see as frightening, dangerous or spoiled in some way. This would provide additional opportunities to reinforce 'keeping safe' messages and warnings about potentially dangerous places in the locality.

Ask the children to think about the special places which pets choose for themselves, especially the places where they sleep or go to escape from people. What makes these places special for each pet? How do pets behave if they can't have their special places, or if someone disturbs them or spoils their special place? How do the children feel when someone takes over or spoils their special places, or makes them feel unsafe there? Encourage the children to take this further and look at how other people might feel if their special places are spoilt, invaded or changed. Who could people complain to? How would they complain?

Our pets' special places

Our cat gets into boxes and baskets even if they're too small.

Our budgie likes to sit on my dad's neck.

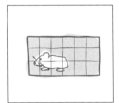

Our hamster hides when he wants to go to sleep.

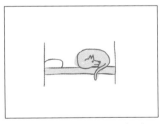

My dog has a special place on my bed. My mum goes mad.

Next door's cat sleeps in our garden on the steps in the sun.

Invite the children to share in the making of a collage of happy places. Help them to bring together illustrations from magazines, photographs and their own drawings and writing. In addition they could help you make a display of books, stories, poems and songs about happy places which they have enjoyed. Conclude this work by looking at what the children think they can do to make places happy or happier.

Me and my relationships

Key words

time line   represent   child   parent   responsibility   independent   caring   love

Content box 6

> **6**
>
> ### On a day like today
> *What are the things I do on a day like today on my own? with help? What do I think I would be doing on a day like today if I were a mum or a dad with my own family? What if I were a mum growing a new baby inside me? How are babies cared for before they are ready to be born, and afterwards when they are new? Why do we grow up so slowly? What do we need to learn so we can be good mums and dads?*

Activity 1 *Day after day*

- Talking together. Collecting up and organising ideas into a time line.

- Individual and class work.

Talk with the children about the things they do on a day like today – a school day. Collect up their ideas and organise them as a time line.

we get up → eat → clean teeth → go to school → work → play

go home ← have story ← work ← play ← have dinner

have tea → watch TV → wash → clean teeth → go to sleep

Remind the children that these are things they do for themselves. Ask the children to include all the things they also do for other people.

What a lot we do in a day!

We:

feed the cat   empty the bin   go to the shops

wash up   help people   tidy up

play with the baby   get the tea

You could tell the children about how much they manage to fit into one day. Ask them what they think their day would be like if they were a mum or a dad. Make a shared list.

This is what mums and dads have to do on a day like today:

get the children up	cook and mend things	dig the garden
go to work	feed the cat	do the washing
look after grandma	take the children to school	sort out problems
clean the house	drive the car	make the beds

Ask whether both mums and dads can do all these jobs. Take the opportunity to challenge stereotypical views of gender while respecting cultural mores.

Look at the fact that some mums and dads prefer one kind of job, but can do both. Is there anything that only mums can do?

Tell the children about Michael's (or any other name) family. Michael's mum and dad do all the things the class have described. Michael's dad is a good cook and his mum is good at mending their car. Michael's mum and dad are having a new baby. His mum is growing the baby inside her until it is strong enough to be born.

Talk with the children about the unique role of mums in growing a new baby inside their body until the baby is ready to be born. Reinforce their knowledge that it takes both a man and a woman to make a new baby.

Talk about the hard work involved in looking after a new baby and how, if they were a mum or dad, the children could fit all that work into a day. Remind them that this goes on for a long time.

You need to:

feed the baby   change its nappy   bath it

take it for a walk   play with it   dress it

teach it   love it   keep it safe

You could contrast this with animals whose young are soon independent.

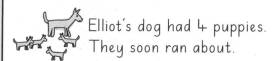 Elliot's dog had 4 puppies. They soon ran about.

 Hanif has a rabbit. It's having babies again. It doesn't take long.

 Michelle's mum is having twins. She knows. They took a picture inside her. They won't be born for a long time.

Remind the children that they are growing up slowly because there is such a lot to learn before they can become mums and dads themselves and help their children be healthy, safe and happy.

Reflection and action

Look back with the children at all they have learned about getting on well with friends, family, people at school and all the people special to them.
- Remind them that they are special to many people in many different ways.
- Talk with them about their progress in being able to recognise how they are feeling and tell people this. Remind them that this is an important part of their happiness now and will be important while they are growing up.
- Remind them that there are things that they and other people treasure and the importance of respecting these things. Recall the importance of caring not only for people but for places, and remind them that there are rules and laws about places and how people behave there. Can they remember their 'everywhere' rule?
- Look back at the work they did about growing up. Remind them that babies and children need a lot of time, love and help to grow up happily and safely, and that one day they may decide to be parents. Remind them that girls grow up to be women and boys grow up to be men and that they can then decide they want to make a baby with someone they love.
- Ask them to practise caring for themselves and other people.

Ages 4 to 7

Sensitive Issues

Activity Sheets

Key themes

Activity sheets

The 30 activity sheets on the following pages have been designed to reinforce and extend the key messages and concepts the children explore as they work through the Sensitive Issues themes in *Health for Life*. The activity sheets are not tied in to specific lesson plans, but can be used as appropriate.

Differentiation

The activity sheets can be used in a variety of ways to respond to the differing needs of the children and their growing skills in working with more formal tasks. From your knowledge of the classes you teach you will be able to judge when to use a particular activity sheet to reinforce and consolidate their learning.

Children who have finished working through an activity sheet will find that there is an instruction given at the bottom of the page to turn the paper over and carry out an additional activity.

Introducing the activity sheets

You may decide to begin by introducing an activity sheet to the whole class, working with them to explore the task and discuss the content. You could look at, and establish their understanding of, the vocabulary provided in the word box at the top of each sheet and encourage them to extend this.

You could follow up this shared approach by asking some children to work through the activity sheet on their own, in pairs or in small groups, thus allowing for further differentiation.

Format

There is a variety of activities on the sheets, including drawing and writing. The children are helped by a recognisable format and a simple repeated language of instruction.

Help with vocabulary and spelling

At the top of each activity sheet there is a useful word box which can be used for different purposes according to the children's needs. Explain to the children that they can use the words in this box as: a spelling check; a starting point or clue for responding to the task; a means of checking that they have included everything they can in their answers.

You may decide it would be helpful to add to the word box for individual children, especially those taking the first steps in writing for themselves, or to provide a list of more challenging words and phrases to extend a more able group.

As the children finish their work they can be asked to read through what they have written. They can do this individually to encourage them to self-correct. Some children could be ready to work in pairs for this review and in this way extend their skills of constructive criticism.

At the end of each activity sheet the children are required to evaluate the effort they have put into their piece of work and to tick the appropriate box:

I worked my hardest. ☐
I could have worked harder. ☐
I will next time. ☐

You may wish to encourage the children to take their activity sheets home so that they can share their achievement with their families.

This can be a way of demonstrating, in a simple and clear way, the focus of the teaching and learning in an important aspect of the curriculum, that of their child's present and future health and wellbeing.

Activity Sheet 1

What goes onto *my* body?

Name _____ **Date** _____

Word box

| clothes, | shoes, | cream, | plasters, | dirt, | germs |

Draw yourself with some of the things that go **onto** your body.
One is done for you.

hat

copy

This is my body.

T _____

These are safe to put onto my body:

_____

These are <u>not</u> safe to put onto my body:

_____

On the back of this paper **draw** two things that are **not** safe to put onto your body.
Write what they are.

Tick ✔ the true box.	
I worked my hardest.	☐
I could have worked harder.	☐
I will next time.	☐

The world of drugs
Health for Life 1 Text © Noreen Wetton and Trefor Williams 2000 Illustrations © Nelson 2000 Published by Thomas Nelson and Sons Ltd

Activity Sheet 2 # What goes into *my* body?

Name _____ **Date** _____

Word box

medicines, food, drinks, dust, dirt, bee stings, smoke, smells, noise, sharp things

Draw yourself with some of the things that go **into** your body.
One is done for you.

cakes

copy
This is my body.

T _____

These are safe to put into my body:

_____

These are <u>not</u> safe to put into my body:

_____

On the back of this paper **draw** two things that are **not** safe to put into your body.
Write what they are.

Tick ✔ the true box.
I worked my hardest. ☐
I could have worked harder. ☐
I will next time. ☐

The world of drugs
Health for Life 1 Text © Noreen Wetton and Trefor Williams 2000 Illustrations © Nelson 2000 Published by Thomas Nelson and Sons Ltd

Activity Sheet 3   *Who decides?*

Name _____ Date _____

Word box
medicines, drugs, drinks, food, dust, smoke, germs, injections, music

Here are some things that go **into** your body.
Can you draw them?

sweets	dirt	fresh air
ice cream	smells	medicines

Here are some ways that things get into your body.
Add more things to each box.

I put these in	**These get in by themselves**	**Someone tells me to**
cakes	insect bites	medicines

On the back of this paper **draw** two things that are **not** safe to put into your body.
Write what they are.

Tick ✔ the true box.	
I worked my hardest.	☐
I could have worked harder.	☐
I will next time.	☐

The world of drugs
Health for Life 1 Text © Noreen Wetton and Trefor Williams 2000 Illustrations © Nelson 2000 Published by Thomas Nelson and Sons Ltd

Activity Sheet 4 | *Smoking*

Name _____ **Date** _____

Word box

smell,   smoke,   don't,   like,   dangerous,   harm,   drugs

Draw someone smoking a cigarette.

Draw yourself in the picture.

What are you saying?

I am saying

On the back of this paper **draw** someone saying:

Do you want a puff of my cigarette?

What would you say to them?

Write: I would say _____

Tick ✔ the true box.

I worked my hardest. ☐

I could have worked harder. ☐

I will next time. ☐

The world of drugs
Health for Life 1   Text © Noreen Wetton and Trefor Williams 2000 Illustrations © Nelson 2000   Published by Thomas Nelson and Sons Ltd

PHOTOCOPIABLE

Activity Sheet 5 *Is it safe?*

Name _____ Date _____

Word box

grown-up, told, asked, picked up, touched, left, gave, showed, injection

Josh found a lunch box in the playground.

Draw what Josh did with the lunch box.

Was this a safe thing to do?

Yes, because _____

_____

No, because _____

_____

Shadi found some money on the way to school.

Draw what Shadi did with the money.

Was this a safe thing to do?

Yes, because _____

_____

No, because _____

_____

On the back of this paper **draw** yourself finding some medicine. What would you do?

Write: I would _____

Tick ✔ the true box.

I worked my hardest. ☐

I could have worked harder. ☐

I will next time. ☐

The world of drugs
Health for Life 1   Text © Noreen Wetton and Trefor Williams 2000   Illustrations © Nelson 2000   Published by Thomas Nelson and Sons Ltd

Activity Sheet 6 — Do as I say

Name _____ **Date** _____

Word box

read, late, story, tired, dinner, milk, hungry, cuddle, dangerous, tell, drugs

Mum is trying to make Jed go to bed. What is she saying?

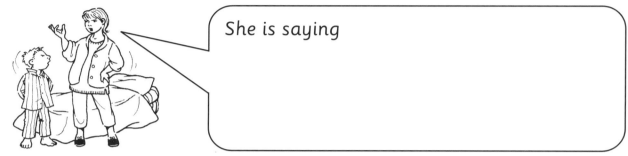

She is saying

Kim is trying to make her cat come in. What is she saying?

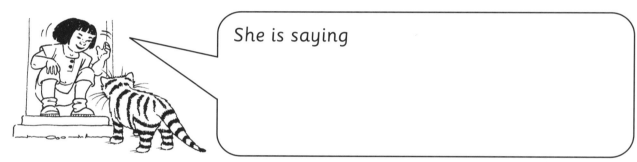

She is saying

Some big children are trying to make Jed and Kim taste some new sweets. What are Jed and Kim saying?

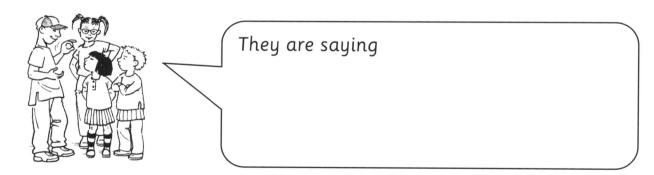

They are saying

On the back of this paper **draw** yourself saying 'No' to someone. Why are you saying 'No'?

Write: *I am saying no because*

_____

Tick ✔ the true box.

I worked my hardest. ☐

I could have worked harder. ☐

I will next time. ☐

The world of drugs

Health for Life 1   Text © Noreen Wetton and Trefor Williams 2000 Illustrations © Nelson 2000   Published by Thomas Nelson and Sons Ltd

Activity Sheet 7   *Persuaders*

Name _____ **Date** _____

Word box

help,   home,   things,   kind,   secrets,   hide,   hurt,   try it,   bully

Here are some good things people try to persuade us to do.
Can you think of some more? Put them in the box.

eat up dinner

keep toys tidy

Here are some dangerous things people try to persuade us to do.
Can you think of some more? Put them in the box.

bully people

not tell

On the back of this paper **draw**
someone trying to persuade you
to do something you know is
dangerous.
What would you say?

Write: I would say _____

Tick ✔ **the true box.**
I worked my hardest.   ☐
I could have worked harder.   ☐
I will next time.   ☐

The world of drugs
Health for Life 1   Text © Noreen Wetton and Trefor Williams 2000 Illustrations © Nelson 2000   Published by Thomas Nelson and Sons Ltd

Activity Sheet 8   *Help! Help!*

Name _____ Date _____

Word box

inhaler, spray, good drug, urgent, worry, stand still, attack, sensible, calm

Dan has asthma.
He is playing in the playground.
He is coughing and can't breathe.
He needs someone to tell the
teacher.

Draw Dan here.

What would you say to Dan?

I would say

What would you say to the teacher to make her come at once?

I would say

On the back of this paper **draw**
yourself telling your family what
happened to Dan.
What are you saying?

Write: 'Guess what? _____'

Tick ✔ the true box.
I worked my hardest.   ☐
I could have worked harder.   ☐
I will next time.   ☐

The world of drugs
Health for Life 1   Text © Noreen Wetton and Trefor Williams 2000   Illustrations © Nelson 2000   Published by Thomas Nelson and Sons Ltd

Activity Sheet 9

A new kind of medicine

Name _____ **Date** _____

Word box

fresh air,   playing outside,   telling someone,   having a rest,   cuddling a teddy,
playing with a friend, making something

Aziz and Lisa have found a new
kind of medicine to make them
better.

What do you think it is?

I think their new medicine is

On the back of this paper draw
yourself doing something to make
yourself feel better.
What are you doing?

Write: I am _____

Tick ✔ the true box.
I worked my hardest. ☐
I could have worked harder. ☐
I will next time. ☐

The world of drugs
Health for Life 1 Text © Noreen Wetton and Trefor Williams 2000 Illustrations © Nelson 2000 Published by Thomas Nelson and Sons Ltd

Sharing the messages

Name _____ Date _____

Word box

only take,   dangerous,   new medicine,   fresh air,   tell,   sensible,   decide

Here is a take home sheet to share with your family.

Dear _____

I have been learning about medicines, drugs and how they can make us better.

This is my message about medicines and drugs.

This is my message about getting better.

This is my message to people who try to persuade us.

You can ask me some more about our work or come to our classroom and see what we have done.

Love from _____

PHOTOCOPIABLE

Activity Sheet 1   *Safe in my home*

Name _____ **Date** _____

Word box
family, mum, dad, brother, sister, don't touch, stay, play, hot, run, listen, stop and think

Draw your home.

copy

This is my home.

T _____

Who keeps you safe in your home?

_____

_____

What do you do to keep yourself safe in your home?

I _____

and I _____

On the back of this paper **draw** yourself playing outside your home. What are you doing to keep yourself safe?

Write: I am _____

Tick ✔ the true box.
I worked my hardest. ☐
I could have worked harder. ☐
I will next time. ☐

Keeping myself safe
Health for Life 1   Text © Noreen Wetton and Trefor Williams 2000   Illustrations © Nelson 2000   Published by Thomas Nelson and Sons Ltd

Activity Sheet (2) # *Safe indoors*

Name _____ **Date** _____

Word box

| kettle, | hot, | stairs, | fire, | cooker, | things falling |

Jo is thinking about things she needs to keep safe from at home. Can you think of some more? Put them in the boxes.

At home, I keep safe from:	
the hot iron	doors that slam

Draw yourself keeping safe on the stairs.

copy

I am careful when

I

_____

I go up and down

_____

the stairs.

_____

On the back of this paper **draw** yourself keeping safe at school. What are you doing?

Write: *I am* _____

Tick ✔ the true box.

I worked my hardest. ☐

I could have worked harder. ☐

I will next time. ☐

Keeping myself safe
Health for Life 1   Text © Noreen Wetton and Trefor Williams 2000   Illustrations © Nelson 2000   Published by Thomas Nelson and Sons Ltd

Activity Sheet 3) *Safe outdoors*

Name _____ Date _____

Word box

road,   cars,   fast,   swings,   gate,   sharp things,   people

Sam is playing with a friend outdoors. Draw them keeping safe.

> copy

They are keeping safe outdoors.

T _____

Draw three things they are keeping safe from.

They are keeping safe from

_____

They are keeping safe from

_____

They are keeping safe from

_____

On the back of this paper **draw** you and your friend playing in a safe place.

Write: It is safe because _____

Tick ✔ the true box.
I worked my hardest.   ☐
I could have worked harder.   ☐
I will next time.   ☐

Keeping myself safe
Health for Life 1   Text © Noreen Wetton and Trefor Williams 2000   Illustrations © Nelson 2000   Published by Thomas Nelson and Sons Ltd

Activity Sheet 4 # *Who is in charge?*

Name _____ **Date** _____

Word box

teacher, helper, driver, crossing patrol, mum, myself, lifeguard, keep rules, listen, stop, think, street

Who is in charge:

in the playground?

_____

at the crossing?

_____

on the bus?

_____

at the park?

_____

on a school trip?

_____

at the swimming pool?

_____

How can you help them?

I can _____

On the back of this paper **draw** yourself outdoors.
Where are you? Who is in charge?

Write: I am _____

Tick ✔ the true box.
I worked my hardest.   ☐
I could have worked harder.   ☐
I will next time.   ☐

Keeping myself safe
Health for Life 1   Text © Noreen Wetton and Trefor Williams 2000 Illustrations © Nelson 2000   Published by Thomas Nelson and Sons Ltd

Activity Sheet 5

My keeping safe rules

Name _____ **Date** _____

Word box

stop, use, think, listen, wait, crossing, fast, seatbelt, wash, eating

Rules help us to keep ourselves safe.
Write some rules to help you keep safe.

This is my rule for keeping safe near traffic	Draw yourself keeping this rule
_____ _____ _____	

This is my rule for keeping safe in the classroom	Draw yourself keeping this rule
_____ _____ _____	

This is my rule for keeping healthy	Draw yourself keeping this rule
_____ _____ _____	

On the back of this paper **draw** yourself in a car.
Write your rule for keeping safe in a car.

Tick ✔ the true box.

I worked my hardest. ☐
I could have worked harder. ☐
I will next time. ☐

Keeping myself safe
Health for Life 1 Text © Noreen Wetton and Trefor Williams 2000 Illustrations © Nelson 2000 Published by Thomas Nelson and Sons Ltd

Activity Sheet 6 — *Take care!*

Name _____ **Date** _____

Word box
other people, rough, stop, think, share, turn, fair, selfish, dangerous, hurt, tell

Draw these children in the playground.

Mandy is running and bumping into other children.	Ben is playing ball with his special friend. He won't let other children join in.	Toby is playing 'chase'. He makes all the rules so he wins.

What would you say to these children about keeping safe in the playground?

Mandy,

Ben,

Toby,

There is a bully in the playground.
On the back of this paper **draw** yourself keeping safe from the bully.
What are you doing to keep safe?

Write: I am _____

> **Tick ✔ the true box.**
> I worked my hardest. ☐
> I could have worked harder. ☐
> I will next time. ☐

Keeping myself safe
Health for Life 1   Text © Noreen Wetton and Trefor Williams 2000   Illustrations © Nelson 2000   Published by Thomas Nelson and Sons Ltd

Activity Sheet 7) *Stop and think!*

Name _____ Date _____

Tom is playing in the kitchen on his own, keeping safe.

Draw Tom here.

What is he doing?

Tom is _____

Tom's mum has come into the kitchen.

Draw Tom with his mum.

What is Tom's mum saying?

She is saying

How does Tom feel?

He feels _____

_____

On the back of this paper **write** a rule for keeping safe in the kitchen.

Tick ✔ the true box.
I worked my hardest. ☐
I could have worked harder. ☐
I will next time. ☐

Keeping myself safe
Health for Life 1 Text © Noreen Wetton and Trefor Williams 2000 Illustrations © Nelson 2000 Published by Thomas Nelson and Sons Ltd

Activity Sheet 8 — *Danger ahead!*

Name _____ **Date** _____

Word box

stupid, foolish, won't, sensible, take care, protect, tell, grown-up, decide, hurt, allowed

---

Draw someone trying to make you do something dangerous.	What would you say? *I would say* What would you do? *I would* _____ _____

Draw someone asking you to get in their car to find their puppy.	What would you say? *I would say* What would you do? *I would* _____ _____

On the back of this paper **draw** yourself watching TV.
Something scary comes on.
What would you do?

Write: *I would* _____

Tick ✔ the true box.

I worked my hardest. ☐

I could have worked harder. ☐

I will next time. ☐

Keeping myself safe
Health for Life 1 Text © Noreen Wetton and Trefor Williams 2000 Illustrations © Nelson 2000 Published by Thomas Nelson and Sons Ltd

PHOTOCOPIABLE

Activity Sheet 9 *Everywhere rules*

Name _____ Date _____

Word box
feed, ducks, can't, swim, sensible, dangerous, know, better, crossing patrol

Here is a rule for keeping safe in the park.

> Keep away from the pond.

Is it a good rule? Yes, because _____

No, because _____

Here is a rule for keeping safe at the seaside.

> Always keep your sunhat and T-shirt on.

Is it a good rule? Yes, because _____

No, because _____

Here is a rule for keeping safe on the way to school.

> Cross the road where you think it is safe.

Is it a good rule? Yes, because _____

No, because _____

On the back of this paper **write** an **everywhere** rule to help keep you safe wherever you are.

> **Tick ✔ the true box.**
> I worked my hardest. ☐
> I could have worked harder. ☐
> I will next time. ☐

Keeping myself safe
Health for Life 1 Text © Noreen Wetton and Trefor Williams 2000 Illustrations © Nelson 2000 Published by Thomas Nelson and Sons Ltd

Sharing the messages

PHOTOCOPIABLE

Name _____ Date _____

Word box

know, sensible, listen, dangerous, stop, think, hurt, people, decide, in charge

Here is a take home sheet to share with your family.

Dear _____

I have been learning about keeping myself safe.

This is my message about keeping safe in the house.

This is my message about keeping safe outdoors.

This is my **everywhere** rule.

You can ask me some more about our work or come to our classroom and see what we have done.

Love from _____

Keeping myself safe
Health for Life 1 Text © Noreen Wetton and Trefor Williams 2000 Illustrations © Nelson 2000 Published by Thomas Nelson and Sons Ltd

Activity Sheet 1 *Special people*

Name _____ **Date** _____

Word box

mum,   dad,   friend,   baby,   Grandma,   kind,   loving,   good,   very

Draw your family.

> **copy**
> My family is special.
>
> M _____
>
> _____
>
> _____
>
> _____

Draw some more special people.

> **copy**
> These are my special people.
>
> T _____

Who are your special people?

My special people

are _____

_____

_____

_____

On the back of this paper **draw** yourself.
Who says that **you** are special?

Write: _____ says I am special.

Tick ✔ the true box.	
I worked my hardest.	☐
I could have worked harder.	☐
I will next time.	☐

Me and my relationships
Health for Life 1 Text © Noreen Wetton and Trefor Williams 2000 Illustrations © Nelson 2000 Published by Thomas Nelson and Sons Ltd

Activity Sheet 2   *Feeling good*

Name _____ **Date** _____

Word box

playing with friends,   games,   helping,   eating,   sharing,   having fun

Draw yourself feeling good.

> **copy**
> This is me. I feel good.
>
> T_____

What are you doing?

I am _____

_____

_____

_____

Draw yourself making your friend feel good.

What are you doing?

I am _____

_____

_____

_____

On the back of this paper **draw** your friend making **you** feel good. What is your friend doing?

Write: My friend is _____

Tick ✔ the true box.

I worked my hardest. ☐

I could have worked harder. ☐

I will next time. ☐

Me and my relationships
Health for Life 1 Text © Noreen Wetton and Trefor Williams 2000 Illustrations © Nelson 2000 Published by Thomas Nelson and Sons Ltd

Activity Sheet 3   *Hurt feelings*

Name _____ **Date** _____

Word box
listening, talking, find, grown-up, helping, take care, playing, telling, saying

Someone has hurt Max's feelings.
Draw yourself doing something to make Max feel better.

copy This is me helping Max to feel better. T_____ _____

What are you doing
to help Max feel
better?

I am _____

_____

_____

_____

Draw a little child crying because it is lost.

What are you doing
to make the little
child feel better?

I am _____

_____

_____

_____

Someone has hurt your feelings.
On the back of this paper **draw**
yourself telling someone.
What are you saying?

Write: *I am saying* _____

Tick ✔ the true box.
I worked my hardest.   ☐
I could have worked harder.   ☐
I will next time.   ☐

Me and my relationships
Health for Life 1   Text © Noreen Wetton and Trefor Williams 2000   Illustrations © Nelson 2000   Published by Thomas Nelson and Sons Ltd

Activity Sheet 4   *Feeling better*

Name _____ **Date** _____

Word box

upset, scared, worried, cross, saying, listening, told, someone, grown-up, don't

---

Sam lost his dinner money.
Draw Sam here.

How does Sam feel?

Sam feels _____

_____

Emma forgot her PE kit.
Draw Emma here.

How does Emma feel?

Emma feels _____

_____

Draw yourself feeling upset.

What made you feel upset?

_____

_____

What made you feel better?

_____

_____

On the back of this paper **draw** yourself helping someone to feel better.
What are you saying?
Write: I am saying _____

Tick ✔ the true box.

I worked my hardest. ☐

I could have worked harder. ☐

I will next time. ☐

Activity Sheet 5 *Best friends*

Name _____ Date _____

Word box
play together, talk, love, share, listen, trust, quarrel, upset, used to, make up, sorry

Sandy and Joey are best friends. Draw them here.

What do best friends do?

Best friends _____

_____

What do best friends never do?

Best friends never _____

_____

One day Sandy and Joey stopped being friends.
What do you think happened?

I think _____

How do you think they feel now?

I think they feel _____

because _____

They want to be best friends again. What must they do?

They must _____

On the back of this paper **draw** Sandy and Joey making friends again.
What are they saying?

Write: They are saying _____

Tick ✔ the true box.
I worked my hardest. ☐
I could have worked harder. ☐
I will next time. ☐

Me and my relationships
Health for Life 1 Text © Noreen Wetton and Trefor Williams 2000 Illustrations © Nelson 2000 Published by Thomas Nelson and Sons Ltd

Activity Sheet 6 — *Big brother Bill*

Name _____ **Date** _____

Word box

worried, jealous, look after, playing, watch, listen, amuse, happy, excited, surprised, bring things, nappies

Bill has no brothers or sisters.
Draw Bill here.

Bill's mum is going to have a new baby.
How does Bill feel?

I think Bill feels _____

_____

_____

My list for Bill

How to help with a new baby.

You could _____

_____

You could _____

_____

I think your Mum would feel _____

because _____

Here is Bill's new baby.

Bill wants to help with the new baby.

What can Bill do?

Make a list to help Bill.

On the back of this paper **draw** Bill with the new baby.
What are they doing?

Write: They are _____

Tick ✔ the true box.
I worked my hardest. ☐
I could have worked harder. ☐
I will next time. ☐

Me and my relationships
Health for Life 1 Text © Noreen Wetton and Trefor Williams 2000 Illustrations © Nelson 2000 Published by Thomas Nelson and Sons Ltd

Activity Sheet 7   # *Showing love*

Name _____   **Date** _____

Word box
love,   play,   touch,   listen,   stroke,   cuddle,   gently,   talk,   give

Lucy has a rabbit.
How does Lucy show she loves her rabbit?

She _____

_____

> Draw Lucy with her rabbit.

Jack is with his mum.
How does Jack show he loves his mum?

He _____

_____

> Draw Jack with his mum.

Anna and Harry's grandma is very old.
How do they show that they love their grandma?

They _____

_____

> Draw Anna and Harry with their grandma.

On the back of this paper **draw** yourself with a new baby.
How would you touch a new baby to show you love it?

Write: I would _____

> **Tick ✔ the true box.**
> I worked my hardest.   ☐
> I could have worked harder.   ☐
> I will next time.   ☐

Me and my relationships
Health for Life 1   Text © Noreen Wetton and Trefor Williams 2000   Illustrations © Nelson 2000   Published by Thomas Nelson and Sons Ltd

Activity Sheet 8 # Moving on

Name _____ **Date** _____

Word box

sad, worried, unhappy, upset, scared, strange, write, phone, meet, weekends, cheer up, brave

Kevin is moving house.
He is leaving his school and going
to a new school.

Draw Kevin here.

How do you think Kevin feels?

I think Kevin feels _____

_____

How do you think Kevin's friends feel?

I think Kevin's friends feel _____

_____

What can Kevin do to remember his friends?

Kevin can _____

_____

On the back of this paper **draw**
Kevin going to his new school.
How does he feel now?

Write: *He feels* _____

Tick ✔ the true box.	
I worked my hardest.	☐
I could have worked harder.	☐
I will next time.	☐

Me and my relationships
Health for Life 1 Text © Noreen Wetton and Trefor Williams 2000 Illustrations © Nelson 2000 Published by Thomas Nelson and Sons Ltd

Activity Sheet 9 # *Something sad*

Name _____ **Date** _____

Word box

upset, unhappy, crying, remember, loving, playing, stroking, comfort, friend, long time, listening, sharing, sadness

Pat's cat died yesterday. How does Pat feel?

Pat feels _____ because _____

_____

Draw yourself with Pat.

What are you saying to help Pat feel better?

I am saying

What are you doing to help Pat feel better?

I am _____

Something sad has happened to you. On the back of this paper **draw** yourself telling your friend. What is your friend saying and doing to make you feel better?

Write: My friend is _____

Tick ✔ the true box.
I worked my hardest. ☐
I could have worked harder. ☐
I will next time. ☐

Me and my relationships
Health for Life 1 Text © Noreen Wetton and Trefor Williams 2000 Illustrations © Nelson 2000 Published by Thomas Nelson and Sons Ltd

Sharing the messages

Name _____ Date _____

Word box
share, trust, never, listen, look after, cuddle, take care, comfort, understand

Here is a take home sheet to share with your family.

Dear _____

I have been learning about love, friendships and good relationships.

This is my message about best friends.

This is my message about helping people to feel better.

This is my
message
about how
you show
you love people.

You can ask me some more about our work or come to our classroom and see what we have done.

Love from _____

Appendices

Appendix 1

Using the 'Draw and write' techniques

Introduction

- Use the introduction given on the instruction sheet (Appendix 1). Remember not to discuss the topic with the children beforehand.
- Invite the children to draw and write in response to your instructions or questions. You will only be analysing the written statements (though you will find the pictures very illuminating) so it is important to tell the children that there must be some writing at the side of each picture.
- Remind the children who are dictating their captions or statements that it is important on this occasion to whisper to you, so that others cannot hear.
- Tell the children not to colour their pictures until the end of the activity.

Timing

- The activity should be completed in one session. This can vary from 20–30 minutes, depending on the age of the class.

Research validity

- To ensure the accuracy of the results it is important that what the children produce is, as far as possible, their own unaided work. This is why you should prevent them from sharing their ideas. Emphasise that there are no right or wrong answers. If they need to ask for your help, however, they should whisper to you.

Spelling

- If undue emphasis is placed on spelling, this may detract from or prolong the activity in hand.

Labelling

- It would be helpful when analysing your results to label each child's paper with their sex and year group.

Materials

- One A4 sheet of plain paper.

Healthy Lifestyles

A picture of health: part 1

A 'draw and write' activity for children aged 4 to 7

Instructions for carrying out the 'A picture of health' investigation.

Spoken instructions	Reminders
Introduction 'Good morning/Hello. How are you all today? Good, I thought you all looked very well and very healthy. Let me have another look at you. Show me how healthy you are. Yes, a very healthy class.'	Please don't use any other words, for example 'fit and healthy', 'strong', 'feeling good'.
Activity 1: Explanation 'Now I want you to have a good think about all the things you do to make you healthy. No, don't tell me or anyone else. Keep it a secret inside your head. Think of yourself doing things to make you healthy and keep you healthy.	Please don't give any clues or hints. Don't let the children divulge their ideas to others.
Activity 2: Drawing 'Now I want you to go to your places and draw yourself looking healthy and doing all the things you thought of to make you healthy and keep you healthy.' 'If you're not sure how to start, draw yourself looking healthy and then think of things you do to make you healthy.'	Discourage the children from looking at each other's work and discussing their drawings. Don't suggest what to draw. Beware of children copying each other at each stage.
Activity 3: Writing 'Now write what you are doing in your pictures. Whisper if you need me to help with spellings. If you can't write, I'll come round and write for you. You tell me in a whisper and I'll write it for you.'	Don't suggest to the child how his or her picture might be linked to health. Ask only permitted questions. Check that there is something written for each picture each child has drawn. Make sure that each response sheet is marked with child's sex and age or year.

'Now turn your paper over for part 2.'

A picture of health: part 2

Activity 1 'Think about all the people whose job it is to make you healthy and keep you healthy.'

Activity 2 'Draw these people and write at the side of them who each of them is.'

Activity 3 'Look at all these people and put a ring around the one you think is the most important for keeping you healthy.'

Thank the children for taking part.

Any child who has finished could colour in the pictures, *but* beware of them starting to talk while doing this.

Appendix 1

Sensitive Issues

The world of drugs

A 'draw and write' activity for children aged 4 to 7

Instructions for carrying out 'The world of drugs' investigation.

Spoken instructions	Reminders	Beware
'Good morning/Hello. I am going to read you the beginning of a story and then I am going to ask you to draw and write some of your ideas about the people in the story and what they did.'	Remind the children to listen to the story carefully.	Don't mention the word 'drugs' before it appears in the story. Do *not* give any explanation of drugs, for example do not say medicines. The purpose is to find out children's explanations.
Introduce the activity. (See page 234.) Give suitable names to the children mentioned in the introduction.	Read the introduction twice if you think this is appropriate to your class.	Don't let the children comment out loud, or ask questions. Don't let them share their ideas with others. Don't give them any hints or clues.
Ask the questions on page 234 one at a time, asking the children to draw their answers, and to explain them in writing. Make your own decision about how many questions to ask the class. Ask the children to number their responses.	Remind the children that there are no wrong answers and that all their ideas are right. Remind them to draw and write every time, and to write as much as they like. (The written responses are the ones which are analysed.) Tell them to leave colouring until later.	
Conclusion 'Now let's stop. I am going to read the questions through again. Make sure you have numbered them.' 'Make sure you have some writing by every drawing.'	A two or five minute warning is useful. Some children may need your help to number their responses.	Look out for children who spend too much time colouring their pictures and do not write. Remind them *not* to put their names on their papers.

Appendix 1

The world of drugs – the invitation and questions

1	4
2	5
3	6
	7

☐ Girl   ☐ Boy   ☐ Year

Response Sheets

Note It can be helpful to have some response sheets prepared to make the children's task and the analysis easier.

1 Introduce the activity to the children:
'A child was walking home when s/he found a bag with drugs inside it. Draw what you think was in the bag. If you can, write at the side what it is you have drawn. If you can't write, whisper to me what it is you have drawn and I will write it for you.'

Next, ask the children to continue drawing and writing in response to the following questions and instructions. Not all of these will be appropriate for all the children. You know your children and will be able to make your own decision about where to stop.

2 'Who do you think lost the bag? Draw the person. If you can, write at the side who it is you have drawn. If not, whisper to me and I will write it for you. What kind of person is this?'

3 'Draw and write about what you think that person was going to do with the bag.'

4 'Draw and write about what the child did with the bag.'

5 'What would you have done if you had found it? Draw and write what you would have done.'

6 'Can a drug be good for you? Can it help you? If so, when? Draw and write about it.'

7 'Can a drug be bad for you? Or hurt you? If so, when? Draw and write about it.'

('The world of drugs' in research strategy has been used by many schools, nationally and internationally and has become known as *Jugs and Herrings*. In the original research some 4 year olds interpreted 'drugs' as 'jugs', and many older children interpreted 'heroin' as 'herring'.)

It is important that the children know that they are responding anonymously. It is particularly important to check that there are no named response sheets when you intend to share your findings with others.

Appendix 1

Keeping myself safe

A 'draw and write' activity for children aged 4 to 7

Instructions for carrying out the 'Keeping myself safe' investigation with the children

Spoken instructions	Permitted prompts and reminders	Beware
'Good morning/Hello. It's good to find you have all got here safely. Today I want you to think about all the things you have to keep safe from, and how you keep yourself safe indoors and outdoors. Don't tell me or anyone about them. Keep them in your head until we are ready to draw and write.'	'There are no wrong answers. All your ideas are right.' 'Think about keeping safe wherever you are and wherever you go, indoors and outdoors.'	Don't mention danger, dangerous people, places or things. Don't mention any recent accidents.
Invite the children to draw and write in response to the questions on page 236, working through them one at a time and numbering them as they do.	Tell the children they can draw as many pictures as they wish. Remind them that every drawing must have some writing alongside it but to leave colouring until later. Remind them that they are thinking about *what* they are keeping safe from and *how* they are keeping safe.	Don't let the children comment out loud, or ask questions. Don't let them share their ideas with others. Don't give them any hints or clues.
Conclusion Remind the children that every drawing must have some writing alongside it. Ask the children to label their response sheets: *Indoors* on the front, and *Outdoors* on the back. You could write these two words on the board.	Remind the children that there are no wrong answers and that all their ideas are right. Remind them to draw and write every time and to write as much as they like. (The written responses are the ones which are analysed.)	Look out for children who spend too much time colouring their pictures and do not write. Remind them *not* to put their names on their papers.

Appendix 1

Keeping myself safe – the invitation and questions

1	4
2	5
3	6
	7
	☐ Girl ☐ Boy ☐ Year

Response Sheets

Note It can be helpful to have some response sheets prepared to make the children's task and the analysis easier.

1 Ask the children to 'Draw yourself indoors keeping yourself safe'.

2 While they are drawing, ask them to stop and think about the following question:

'What are you keeping yourself safe from? Draw and write about all the things you are keeping safe from. If you need help with spellings or writing, whisper to me and I will help you.'

3 Ask the children to think about this question:

'How are you keeping yourself safe? Write down how you are keeping safe. If you need help with the writing, whisper to me and I will write for you.'

4 Ask the children to turn the paper over and draw themselves keeping safe outdoors.

5 Repeat question 2.

6 Repeat question 3.

7 Finally ask them to draw and write in response to the question: 'Whose job is it to keep you safe wherever you are?'

It is important that the children know that they are responding anonymously. It is particularly important to check that there are no named response sheets when you intend to share your findings with others.

Appendix 1

Me and my relationships
A 'draw and write' activity for children aged 4 to 7

Instructions for carrying out the 'Me and my relationships' investigation with the children

Spoken instructions	Permitted prompts and reminders	Beware
'Good morning/Hello. Today I want you to think about the people who are very special to you. Don't tell me or anyone about them. Keep it in your head until we're ready to draw and write.'	'There are no wrong answers. All your ideas are right.' 'They can be people in your family or other people who are special to you.'	Don't mention terms such as 'love', 'care for', 'care about', 'take care of', 'relationships'.
Invite the children to draw and write in response to the questions on page 238, working through them one at a time and numbering them as they do. Make your own decision about how many questions to ask the class.	Remind the children they are thinking about *their* special people. Remind them to leave colouring until later.	Don't let the children comment out loud, or ask questions. Don't let them share their ideas with others. Don't give them any hints or clues.
Conclusion Remind the children that every drawing must have some writing alongside it. Ask the children to make sure they have numbered their responses.	Remind the children that there are no wrong answers and that all their ideas are right. Remind them to draw and write every time, and to write as much as they like. (The written responses are the ones which are analysed.) Make sure that each response sheet is marked with the child's sex and age or year.	Look out for children who spend too much time colouring their pictures and do not write. Remind them *not* to put their names on their papers.

Appendix 1

Me and my relationships – the invitation and questions

1	5
2	6
3	7
4	8 ☐ Girl ☐ Boy ☐ Year

Response Sheets

Note It can be helpful to have some response sheets prepared to make the children's task and the analysis easier.

Ask the children to draw and write in response to these instructions:

1 'Draw the people who are special to you. If you can, write down who they are. If you can't write, whisper to me and I will write for you.'

2 'Draw what you do to make them happy. Write down how you make them happy. If you can't write, whisper to me and I will write for you.'

3 'Draw what you do to make them cross. Write down how you make them cross. If you can't write, whisper to me and I will write for you.'

The following questions will not be appropriate for all the children. You know your children and will be able to make your own decision about where to stop. Some children may prefer to draw first and add their written answers afterwards.

4 'What is the happiest thing you can remember? Write it down. If you can't, I will help you.'

5 'What is the saddest thing you can remember? Write it down. If you can't, I will help you.'

6 'Write down the things you like about your best friend.'

7 'Write down the things your best friend likes about you.'

8 'What do people do to make you happy?'

It is important that the children know that they are responding anonymously. It is particularly important to check that there are no named response sheets when you intend to share your findings with others.

Appendix 2

A brief history of health education

This is a brief historical background which attempts to link the past with the present in order to illuminate an absorbing legacy left to us by our forebears concerning their search for the blessings of health. The search is both a long and absorbing story but, as yet, too little known. It is clear from numerous historical papers and records that health education in some shape or form has existed ever since human beings settled and lived in social groups. For example 'The Code of Hammurabi', formulated around 1900 BC by Hammurabi the great king of Babylon, governed the conduct of physicians and ensured good health practices by his people.

Perhaps the oldest and most famous health education tract, advocating moderation in the use of alcohol, was written in Egypt about 1000 BC. Its message is timeless!

> 'Don't drink yourself helpless in the beer garden. You speak and you don't know what you are saying. If you fall down and break your limbs, no one will help you and your drinking companions will get up and say "Away with this drunkard".'

The Hebrews, recognising the importance of health-related behaviour, constructed their 'Mosaic Law' which stresses both personal and community responsibility for health and, without knowing much about infectious diseases, they were able to define the conditions unacceptable for healthy living. The Hebrews were responsible for one of the first acts of preventive medicine by segregating lepers from the community – as recorded by Leviticus.

Ancient Greece excelled in the physical aspects of personal health and here the 'harmonious development of the faculties' was the guiding philosophy, and personal strength and fitness was revered. This time was also the origin of systematic medicine and of the famous Hippocratic oath, as well as providing a base for promoting 'wholeness' as an aim of school education. This period has provided us also with the rich legacy of the Olympic Games, where training of body and mind reaches near perfection. Sadly, the destruction of Corinth in 146 BC brought an end to their dominance, and the health skills and knowledge were absorbed into Roman culture.

The Romans differed radically from the Greeks in their philosophy, believing in the overwhelming importance of the state over the individual. Their time was marked by huge feats of engineering, bringing clean water to the population and taking away human waste in their marvellously constructed sewers. Education was also an important part of their agenda, where physical education and personal hygiene played an important part.

After the fall of the Roman Empire, the prevailing perceptions of health were summed up by St. Augustine's (AD 354–430) seemingly definitive statement: 'All diseases are to be ascribed to demons' which was, more or less, the epitaph for the pursuit of health and fitness for the next 1400 years. Because the clergy were the only truly educated class virtually the entire emphasis of the time was on the spiritual aspects of life, with a consequent rejection of the human body. From about AD 476 to 1000, a blanket of smoke and haze seems to have been drawn over history and the development of health education, causing it to be very aptly named 'The Dark Ages'. Western civilisation seemed to be in a state of chaos.

Appendix 2, A brief history of health education cont'd

The six crusades to the Holy Land (AD 1096–1248) are of some interest because of the very brief period of interest in physical fitness and stamina for the wars.

Bubonic plague (The Black Death) struck in 1348, devastating a pathway from Asia to Africa and then northwards through Europe where over 25 million people perished. Some countries later realised that quarantine laws could protect their citizens and Marseilles in France is thought to have been the first city to legally enforce them.

The Renaissance (AD 1453–1600) is associated with a revival of learning in Europe which ushered in a period of real scientific endeavour, leading eventually to a closer understanding of the cause and nature of infectious diseases. By the middle of the 16th century, scholars had differentiated between influenza, smallpox, tuberculosis, bubonic plague and leprosy.

The period 1600–1800 was punctuated by several important events which helped to sustain the steadily developing momentum of health and medical knowledge, research and practice:

- three severe pandemics of bubonic plague in Europe;
- William Harvey's description of the human blood circulation;
- Thomas Sydenham became the first distinguished 'epidemiologist', setting the scene for the development of a new era in scientific medical research;
- Edward Jenner scientifically demonstrated the effectiveness of the smallpox vaccination.

In the 40 years between 1791 and 1831, the population of England and Wales rose from eight to thirteen million, and slowly but surely public health made gains all over Europe and was finally officially recognised in Britain in 1837. Edwin Chadwick made history by publishing a report, 'An inquiry into Sanitary Conditions of the Labouring population of Great Britain' which, among many other facts, reported that 50% of children from working class homes died before they reached their fifth birthday. Similar reports in other European countries finally resulted in the establishing of health education in schools – the first of which is reported to have been in eastern Germany in about the 1850s.

Many schools and hospitals had been established in earlier centuries, mainly through the efforts of religious organisations, and in 1833 a Factory Act was passed that prohibited children under the age of eleven from working more than nine hours a day.

In England, Liverpool was the first city to appoint a medical officer of health (1847) and London was the second (1848). In Europe, doctors were urging their governments to provide for the health of school children, and in 1840 school doctors were appointed to some training colleges in Sweden. Finally, in 1883, the very first school doctor was appointed in Frankfurt-am-Main, Germany. In Britain, the London School Board was the first to appoint a school doctor (1890), and by 1905 school doctors had been appointed by 85 local education authorities and medical inspection of school children was being carried out in 48 areas.

Paradoxically, one of the factors involved in the emergence of health and fitness education in schools was Government's need for fit and healthy soldiers. For example, the need for soldiers to fight in the Boer War at the turn of the 20th century uncovered the unpalatable truth that well over half of those presenting themselves at recruitment centres failed to meet the very modest standards of that time. This, together with the reports from the school doctors on the amount of ill-health, malnutrition and disability among school children, created outcries in Parliament. The Government was motivated to act with great haste to revive standards of health and fitness among children and young people through medical examinations, school meals and health teaching.

A major factor in the health of people in the 20th century has been a slow but steady change from the infection-based diseases (such as tuberculosis, diphtheria, measles, meningitis, scarlet fever, whooping cough, cholera, typhus, and diarrhoea) to those related to patterns of behaviour (such as smoking, dietary problems, lack of exercise, relationship problems, the growing use of illegal substances, teenage pregnancy, and latterly AIDS). The infectious diseases required medical and clinical responses and preventive measures; poor health-related behaviour, on the other hand, needs educational and social science know-how as well as preventive measures. Separate surveys of school health education in Europe in the late 1980s showed that most countries in Europe were attempting some health education in schools, although standards appeared to be low. European countries had been panicked by the scare of illegal drugs, AIDS, heart disease and cancer, and needed to demonstrate their concern by responding through schools.

As the 20th century comes to a close, however, school health education in Europe has become much more research orientated. We have learned that to improve the effectiveness of health education, schools must develop their own plan of action – by putting into practice all that we have learned from research in Europe, Australia and the USA. Research, and indeed common sense, tells us that if classroom-acquired health knowledge, skills and values are to be incorporated into the lifestyles of primary school children, they need first to be confirmed and legitimised by their families, peers, friends and also by wider community approval and support. It is important, therefore, that such work is driven by a desire to equip children with competencies and skills which will enable them to make their own choices and decisions, now and in the future.

Appendix 3

Only a story: *Health for life* and children's literature

In *Health for Life* we have included suggestions for using children's literature as a strategy for reinforcing and extending the key learning skills and competencies. But what makes literature such a valuable strategy for developing learning in aspects of health and citizenship?

Children's literature provides us with an ideal setting in which to tackle those areas of the curriculum which are seen as most sensitive – by parents, schools, communities, and, most importantly, by the children themselves. Our research shows that much of children's sensitivity in these issues comes from their desire to be uniquely themselves, while not appearing to be too different from others. It comes from their need to be valued, and their need to have the confidence and the language to talk about their feelings – their fears, delights, frustrations and hopes – in a secure, non-threatening, listening context. To fulfil these needs, children have to widen their language of feelings: they must be able to go beyond 'mad', 'bad', 'sad' and 'glad', to be able to communicate feelings such as empathy, jealousy, isolation, uncertainty, conflict, remorse, fairness and frustration. Children who experience these feelings without having the language to express them may well be forced to choose other means of expression.

We all know the power of a story, whether it is told or read in the classroom at the close of a day or to a child at bedtime. We know that children are prepared to suspend disbelief and allow themselves to be taken into another world, simply through the power of words. We can all remember, as the story teller, the magical moment of silence before the return to reality, and the cry: 'Read it again!' We know that there are stories which children love to hear over and over again: as if, each time they hear it, there is just a chance that this time it might not turn out the same, that it might just end differently. And yet, if ever we dare to skip a page, to change or miss out just one word, we know we will be pounced on and corrected. Such is the power and magic of the story. As educators we can use that power, without ever spoiling the magic.

When a story is being told in a way that really brings it to life, we find ourselves sharing much more than the narrative. As listeners we share the characters' experiences, their problems, their feelings and the language that they use. We worry for them when we think they are making the wrong decision; we find ourselves wanting to call out to them: 'Look out!' or 'I told you so.' We can laugh, both at them and with them. Often we feel that we are one step ahead of them. Children especially love the sense of superiority in being able to foretell a story's ending before the characters get there; they often know, before the characters do, what they are going to learn about themselves or the world around them. Children will naturally begin to see something of themselves in this world, and it is now that they can, with our help, make the move to beginning to talk about themselves and their own world.

To help children to make this move takes only a few carefully targeted questions. In the safe knowledge that this is really a story about someone else, children will begin to use the language of feelings and relationships with increasing skill and confidence. Now we can help them to find new words and phrases to describe more clearly the feeling someone had at a certain stage of the story. We can close our eyes and try to recreate that feeling, and work out how we would explain it to someone else if it were happening to us: we can *rehearse* putting our feeling into words. We can even come to a fuller understanding of our own feelings and relationships, and be better able, not only to talk about our own concerns, but also to listen empathetically to those of others.

In a story we can get inside other people's lives and lifestyles. We can reflect critically on decisions they make, relate actions to outcomes and think of alternative behaviours which could give the story a different ending. We can see the impact of feelings on behaviour, and of behaviour on feelings. We can do all this because in a story we are being critical about someone else's behaviour, not condemning each other's or our own. We can, if we choose, step further into the story, focusing on a critical moment and asking: 'If you'd been there, hidden from view perhaps, what would you have wanted to say?' or 'If you had been one of these characters, what would you have wanted to do and say, and why?' And we can go beyond this. In a story we can take children into situations where we would never dare to take them in real life: situations fraught with danger, fear and risk; situations physically and emotionally as yet unknown to them. This closeness to reality can be very powerful for the children, but is always tempered by the knowledge that it is *only a story*, happening within a book, and that at any time the book can be closed.

In *Health for Life*, rather than naming specific books or authors, we have chosen to give a more general description of the kinds of story lines and characterisations you might like to use. Our aim has been to help you identify and build up your own resource list: you will know the books which are available in the school, and those that your own different groups of children will get the most from. Sharing your list with others in the school – including the children – will enable you to extend your resource. Whatever literature you choose – story, picture story, extract or poem – there are several different ways in which you can use it:

- **at the beginning of an activity** as a way of taking the children into a situation or raising an issue;
- **within an activity** as a means of demonstrating a risk, raising a new issue or focusing on a skill, or as an example of the language of feelings;
- **as a task** for one group of children, who could read the story or extract for themselves and discuss how it relates to the issue the class has been exploring;
- **as a shared activity** to round off the work done in one or more activities, and reinforce a particular skill or attitude;
- **as a reflective activity** at the end of a theme, as a way of helping the children to bring the varied strands of their learning together.

Of course, much depends on the quality of the piece you have chosen. We have in this country a great heritage of children's literature. We also have, right now, some of the most talented authors and illustrators of children's literature, producing material of the highest quality. In the area of picture storybooks we are currently particularly fortunate. It is sad that some people see picture storybooks as belonging exclusively to the youngest age-range, for they have much to offer older children, precisely because older children are able, with our help, to peel back the 'outer layers' of the story line and discover new depths of meaning.

Each of us will have a personal opinion of what constitutes a good book, and it is difficult to pin down a definition that everyone can agree to. But perhaps one of the best definitions of a good story was given by a child to the librarian in his local library:

> 'Well – it's a story where the people who go in at the beginning come out – sort of different.'

In other words, a story where the characters – human, animal or seemingly inanimate objects – discover, in the course of the story, something new about themselves, other people or the world around them and, in so doing, illuminate the reader's world. Of course, the more powerful the language, the greater the magic the words create, and so the easier it is for children to suspend disbelief and begin to explore the quality of the characters' relationships. In so doing they will be recognising and rehearsing those skills which are crucial to living confident, positive and healthy lifestyles in which they are able to form understandable relationships with other people, their communities and their environments.

One word of warning. Just as children recognise a good story and are prepared to be taken under its spell, so too they can recognise a would-be edifying tale written specifically to put across an issue. It usually takes children about thirty seconds to work out what is being offered, and switch off. We all know the power of a story: we can all appreciate its magic; but we can all spot the lack of it. And children are no different.

Appendix 4

Selected bibliography

Board of Education, *Handbook of Suggestions on Health Education* (H M Stationery Office, 1928)

Department of Health and Science, *The School Health Service 1908–1974* (H M Stationery Office, 1975)

Durkin, K, *Developmental Social Psychology: From Infancy to Old Age* (Blackwell, 1995)

Final Report of Advisory Group on Citizenship, *Education for Citizenship and the Teaching of Democracy in Schools* (1998) (DfEE Publications, 1999)

Goleman, D, *Emotional Intelligence* (Bloomsbury, 1996)

Green, L W and Anderson, C L, *Community Health* (Times Mirror/Mosby College of Publishing, 1986)

Health Education Authority, 'Five Decades of Health Education': *Health Education Journal Vol. 52 no. 3* (1993)

Kolbe, L J, in *Why School Health Education?* – Report of 'Delbert Oberteuffer Centennial Symposium' in Atlanta, Georgia (Association for the Advancement of Health Education, USA, 1985)

McGurk, H and Hurry, J, *Project Charlie: an evaluation of lifeskills drug education programme for primary schools* (Central Drugs Prevention Unit, Home Office, 1995)

Ministry of Health, *Health Education – Report of a Joint Committee of the Central and Scottish Health Services Council* (H M Stationery Office, 1964)

National Foundation For Education Research, *Whole School Healthy School – an essential guide to the health promoting school* (Health Education Authority, 1999)

National Health and Medical Research Council of Australia, *Effective School Health Promotion – Towards Health-promoting Schools* (Australian Government Publishing Service, 1996)

Office of H M Chief Inspector Of Schools in Wales, *Standards and Quality in Personal and Social Education (PSE)* (Hackman Print, 1997)

Report of the National Advisory Group on Personal, Social and Health Education, *Preparing Young People for Adult Life* (DfEE Publications, 1999)

Rubin, J L et al, *Facts and Feelings in the Classroom* (Ward Lock Educational, 1973)

'Saving Lives: Our Healthier Nation', presented to Parliament by the Secretary of State for Health by Command of Her Majesty (The Stationery Office Limited, 1999)